DAKOTAS

DAKOTAS
WHERE THE WEST BEGINS

PHOTOGRAPHS BY PHIL SCHERMEISTER
WRITTEN BY JOHN THOMPSON

NATIONAL GEOGRAPHIC

WASHINGTON, D.C.

CONTENTS

OPPOSITE | *Kenneth Pratt, Jr., competes in men's fancy dancing at the Twin Buttes Powwow in North Dakota.*
PREVIOUS PAGES | *Ranchers round up cattle on a cold May day in Killdeer, North Dakota.* PAGES 6-7 | *Night falls at the junction of the Bad and Missouri Rivers.* PAGES 8-9 | *Summer thunderclouds skim a butte near Regent, North Dakota.*
PAGES 10-11 | *Striped buttes glow at sunset in South Dakota's Badlands National Park.* PAGES 12-13 | *Meadow flowers cluster in a stand of aspens in Black Hills National Forest.*

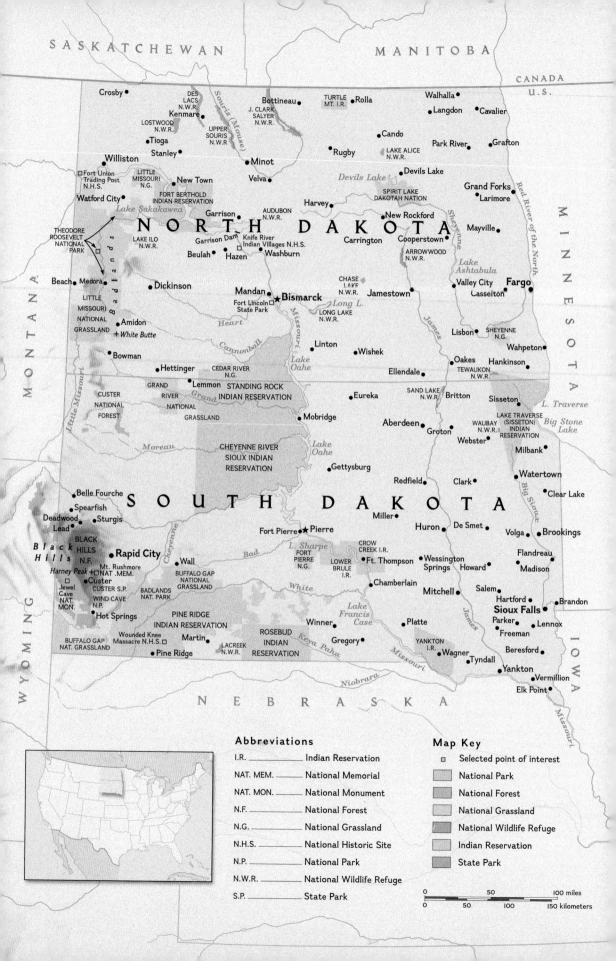

SASKATCHEWAN

MANITOBA

CANADA
U.S.

NORTH DAKOTA

SOUTH DAKOTA

MONTANA

MINNESOTA

WYOMING

IOWA

NEBRASKA

Crosby
DES LACS N.W.R.
Kenmare
Bottineau
TURTLE MT. I.R.
Rolla
Walhalla
Langdon
Cavalier
LOSTWOOD N.W.R.
J. CLARK SALYER N.W.R.
UPPER SOURIS N.W.R.
Souris (Mouse)
Tioga
Stanley
Minot
Cando
Rugby
Park River
Grafton
Williston
Velva
LAKE ALICE N.W.R.
Fort Union Trading Post N.H.S.
LITTLE MISSOURI N.G.
New Town
Devils Lake
Devils Lake
Grand Forks
Larimore
Watford City
Lake Sakakawea
FORT BERTHOLD INDIAN RESERVATION
Harvey
SPIRIT LAKE DAKOTAH NATION
Garrison
AUDUBON N.W.R.
New Rockford
Mayville
THEODORE ROOSEVELT NATIONAL PARK
LAKE ILO N.W.R.
Garrison Dam
Knife River Indian Villages N.H.S.
Carrington
Cooperstown
Sheyenne
Beach
Medora
Badlands
Beulah
Hazen
Washburn
ARROWWOOD N.W.R.
Lake Ashtabula
Valley City
Casselton
Fargo
Dickinson
CHASE LAKE N.W.R.
Mandan
Bismarck
Jamestown
LITTLE MISSOURI NATIONAL GRASSLAND
Fort Lincoln State Park
Long L.
Red River of the North
Amidon
White Butte
Heart
LONG LAKE N.W.R.
Lisbon
SHEYENNE N.G.
Wahpeton
Bowman
Cannonball
Linton
Wishek
Oakes
Hankinson
Hettinger
CEDAR RIVER N.G.
Lake Oahe
Ellendale
TEWAUKON N.W.R.
GRAND RIVER NATIONAL GRASSLAND
Lemmon
STANDING ROCK INDIAN RESERVATION
Eureka
SAND LAKE N.W.R.
Britton
Sisseton
CUSTER NATIONAL FOREST
Little Missouri
Grand
Mobridge
Aberdeen
Groton
WAUBAY N.W.R.
LAKE TRAVERSE (SISSETON) INDIAN RESERVATION
L. Traverse
Big Stone Lake
Moreau
CHEYENNE RIVER SIOUX INDIAN RESERVATION
Lake Oahe
Webster
Milbank
Gettysburg
Belle Fourche
Redfield
Clark
Watertown
Spearfish
Miller
Clear Lake
Deadwood
Sturgis
Huron
De Smet
Volga
Brookings
Lead
Fort Pierre
Pierre
Flandreau
Black Hills
BLACK HILLS N.F.
Rapid City
Wall
CROW CREEK I.R.
Wessington Springs
Howard
Madison
Harney Peak
Mt. Rushmore NAT. MEM.
Bad
FORT PIERRE N.G.
LOWER BRULE I.R.
Ft. Thompson
Salem
Jewel Cave NAT. MON.
Custer
CUSTER S.P.
BUFFALO GAP NATIONAL GRASSLAND
Chamberlain
Mitchell
Hartford
Brandon
WIND CAVE N.P.
White
Sioux Falls
Hot Springs
BADLANDS NAT. PARK
Lake Francis Case
Parker
Lennox
PINE RIDGE INDIAN RESERVATION
Winner
Platte
Freeman
Beresford
BUFFALO GAP NAT. GRASSLAND
Wounded Knee Massacre N.H.S.
Martin
LACREEK N.W.R.
Gregory
Keya Paha
YANKTON I.R.
Wagner
Tyndall
Yankton
Vermillion
Pine Ridge
ROSEBUD INDIAN RESERVATION
Missouri
Elk Point
Niobrara
Big Sioux
James

Abbreviations

I.R. ——— Indian Reservation
NAT. MEM. ——— National Memorial
NAT. MON. ——— National Monument
N.F. ——— National Forest
N.G. ——— National Grassland
N.H.S. ——— National Historic Site
N.P. ——— National Park
N.W.R. ——— National Wildlife Refuge
S.P. ——— State Park

Map Key

▫ Selected point of interest
National Park
National Forest
National Grassland
National Wildlife Refuge
Indian Reservation
State Park

0   50   100 miles
0   50   100   150 kilometers

INTRODUCTION

WHERE DOES THE MIDWEST LEAVE OFF AND THE TRUE WEST begin? One answer would be the Missouri River in the Dakotas. To the east the land lies flat and unbroken. But cross the river and you find yourself in another place entirely. Here the land bulges into hills, blossoms out in buttes and mesas, and twists in dry gullies, as if the smooth carpet of the Midwest ran out of room and had to rumple before it hit the Rockies. In the western Dakotas the landscape is more untamed, the climate drier, the population sparser. Since fewer crops can grow here, ranches are far more common than farms, and with fewer cities the population tends toward the more conservative. West Dakota could have been its own state.

If this is where the West begins, it's also where a large part of the Old West ended. The Plains Indians were the last to succumb to the wave of settlement that washed across the continent, their eagle-feathered war bonnets the last to be packed away in trunks and museum cases. To the Indians, the frontier meant the oncoming front line of settlers. On South Dakota's Wounded Knee Creek the U.S. Army and the Sioux clashed for the last time in 1890. But the American Indian's story continues on and off the Dakotas reservations, their history braided into the flowing stream of modern life.

OPPOSITE | *The Missouri River defines the western Dakotas, where Indian and public lands abound.*
Page 17 | *Eleven-year-old Jake McAlpin learns the art of the lasso.*

We'll meet a number of Native Americans in these pages and hear what they have to tell us about their past and future.

The western Dakotas, then, are a once-and-again frontier, and we start out traveling north along the Missouri River, the same direction Lewis and Clark traveled on their journey of exploration in 1804. Along this fabled avenue to the West stand historic forts, little two-saloon towns, both state capitals, and mile after mile of river shoreline undeveloped save for the edges of giant farms and ranches. The next chapter moves inland to cover the plains, where national grasslands, private land, and Indian reservations form broad, rolling, treeless vistas in earthy palettes of sage greens and taupe browns. On these wide windswept prairies, which sorely tested the early homesteaders, live people with one foot poised in the modern world and one foot firmly in the past.

Chapter 3 takes a look at the most arresting landscape in the western Dakotas—the badlands. These eaten-away sections of the northern plains are like backdrops from Star Wars in their stark and forbidding otherworldliness. Yet mule deer, pronghorn, coyotes, prairie dogs, and other wildlife find refuge here amid banded buttes, steep ravines, and oases of juniper and ash trees. Two national parks highlight the best of the badlands. The final chapter turns to the Black Hills, a pine-swathed eruption of granite peaks and fingerlike spires. Here the land rises into real mountains, topping 7,000 feet. And here again we find the ongoing settlers-versus-Indians story, with a Black Hills twist, as well as the tale of one man's vision to leave his legacy upon a mountain.

Amid all the wide-open space of the western Dakotas live some of the friendliest, most trusting, honest people in the country. Perhaps it's the old frontier help-thy-neighbor spirit, or simply the elbowroom and fresh air. But here under a huge and fathomless sky you still feel the same expansiveness felt by the homesteaders and Plains Indians more than a century ago.

CHAPTER ONE

MISSOURI RIVER

DAKOTA HIGHWAY

There is a place on the Missouri River that few people know about. Even to most residents of central South Dakota, the Narrows—a breathtaking neck of land where the river makes a nearly 360-degree bend—is known only vaguely as the Big Bend area. The fact that it sits on an Indian Reservation helps to keep it isolated, and most road maps show a minor road passing by but not leading to it. There would seem to be no reason to drive out onto this river peninsula. But like so many unheralded spots along the Missouri in the Dakotas, the Narrows rewards those who seek it out (or stumble upon it) with a thrilling sense of discovery and a connection to the earliest explorers who traveled this twisting, bluff-lined, storied waterway.

William Clark used this compass on the 1804-06 Lewis and Clark expedition.
OPPOSITE | *An evening cruise boat plies the Missouri outside Bismarck, North Dakota.*
PREVIOUS PAGES | *Girls prepare to dance at the Twin Buttes Powwow in Twin Buttes, North Dakota.*

Main Street in Chamberlain, South Dakota, bustled with commerce in the early 1800s.
The streets are paved now, but life has not changed much in this small Missouri River town.

THE MISSOURI RIVER SCRAWLS ACROSS the Dakotas like almost legible hand-writing, its script the result of massive sheets of ice that pushed south during the great Ice Age. An ancestral Missouri flowed across Canada, but starting about two million years ago the ice edged south, nosing the river forward. The glacial meltwater carved steep valleys visible today, as well as floored terraces hanging above the floodplain. The river marks the southernmost boundary of those ancient glaciers, and it now divides the Dakotas into eastern and western halves. Some people, in fact, think an East Dakota and a West Dakota would make more sense than a South and North—the western Dakotas, with their rolling, short-grass prairies and badlands, have more in common with

each other than with the flatlands and larger cities east.

The Missouri, then, defines our region, the western Dakotas. Called the Big Muddy by early settlers, it was considered "too thick to drink and too thin to plow." It arcs across southwestern North Dakota in an area called the Missouri Slope and then angles through South Dakota, neatly splitting that state in half, on its 2,540-mile run to the Mississippi. From the mountains of southwest Montana to near St. Louis, the Missouri touches seven states, while draining water from more than half a million square miles—all or part of ten states and two Canadian provinces—in the heart of the continent. All that water moves at a rate of some 76,000 cubic feet per second, though in most places it

looks gentle and inviting. It is the longest river in the United States.

CHAMBERLAIN TO BIG BEND

ON A RECENT TRIP TO THE REGION, I stopped in Chamberlain, South Dakota, where the river measures nearly a mile wide. With the discovery of gold to the west in 1874 and the arrival of the Milwaukee Railroad six years later, the town became a shipping point for east- and west-going passengers and cargo, by both rail and river. Yet with a population of 2,300 it is one of a constellation of small Western towns that seems content to remain small. Its standard three-block main street holds a couple of restaurants, two bars (the Silver Dollar and the Barley Pop Tavern), an old cinema that doubles as a video store, a Radio Shack, a non-touristy jewelry store, a thrift store, and an old-fash-ioned barbershop. Farmers, hunters, and

fishermen keep the town alive. In the fall, hunters go after almost anything that moves—pheasants, prairie chickens, grouse, turkeys, geese, ducks, pronghorn, mule deer, and white-tailed deer.

Chamberlain is also the home of St. Joseph's Indian School, a Catholic board-ing school for Indians dating to 1927. The good intentions of many early reli-gious schools—integrating the Indian into white society—often resulted in wrongheaded attempts to undermine the Indians' culture. Instead of re-educa-tion, St. Joseph's today offers a general curriculum and studies in Lakota lan-guage and culture. The school's Our Lady of the Sioux chapel, for instance, melds both Catholic and Lakota tradi-tions. (Lakota, by the way, is one dialect of the Sioux language, the others being Nakota and Dakota; most Indians in the western Dakotas belong to the Lakota— also called Teton or Western—Sioux tribes.) The chapel is bathed in soft blue light from stained-glass windows depicting both Catholic traditions and sacred Sioux rites: One window represents Benedictines, while another depicts Hanbelcheyapi, or the vision quest.

Perhaps most interesting to visitors is the Akta Lakota Museum, which has a small but up-to-date exhibit area—in the round, Indian-fashion. The beaded moccasins, bison bladder bag, rawhide drum, bison tail flyswatter, bone and wood tools and weapons, all carefully displayed with pertinent information, mostly date from the late 1800s.

Time and again I would see similar items, all from the period when such things went from being mundane objects to cultural artifacts. The transition period from native Americans hunting free-roaming buffalo to a conquered people herded onto reservations is a story you hear over and over in the western Dakotas. Though it is no longer the region's central story, it continues to play out as whites and Indians grapple in legislatures, courtrooms, schoolrooms, and barrooms with the complexities of restitution for past wrongs.

Stained-glass sisterhood in St. Joseph's Indian School chapel.

I stopped by the Barley Pop Tavern one rainy evening and watched a ball game with owner-bartender Will Menke, a goateed young man who took his cap off for the national anthem. Will recently converted the place from a café into a bar, its pressed tin ceiling a vestige of old times. He told me business would pick up later in the fall, with pheasant hunters and dart leagues. The only other customer was a man named Tom Burke, a fund-raiser for St. Joseph's. Some 200 students attend the school, he said, with another 200 on the waiting list. St. Joseph's offers a better education than that available on the reservations, and after eighth grade students are welcome to continue boarding there while attending the local high school. The problem, Tom said, is that too many of the school graduates are still academically behind and would rather go back to the reservation and start having babies.

More discussion followed about the free health care, food, and cell phone service available on the reservations; whether one had to prove one-eighth or one-sixteenth Indian blood to qualify;

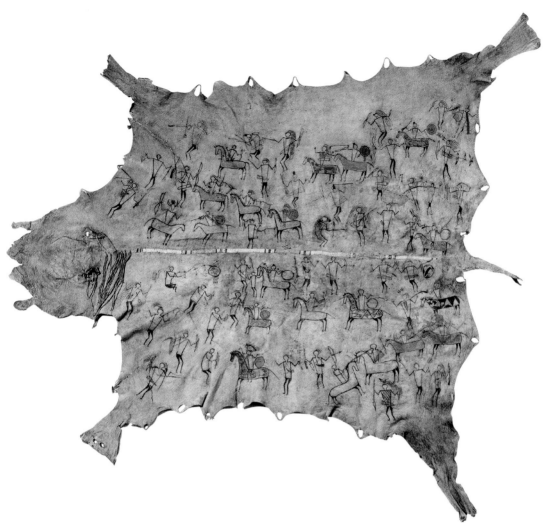

Meriwether Lewis sent this Mandan buffalo robe to Thomas Jefferson in 1805. Many such robes, painted with battle scenes, are displayed in museums throughout the Dakotas; for the Indians, the robes were a way of recording history.

and the high rate of crime and alcoholism on the "rez." Is there a problem fitting in at the local school, I wondered?

"There's no racism here," Tom assured me.

Just up the river on another day, I traveled through the Lower Brule Indian Reservation and met with Sheldon Fletcher, a conservation officer with the reservation's department of fish, wildlife, and recreation. At 36, Sheldon is a big, burly Lakota Indian who claims descent from explorer Meriwether Lewis. He drove me in his pickup, pistol bullets jostling on the panel between seats, to the Narrows of the Big Bend. Gesturing

FOLLOWING PAGES | *Autumn colors burnish the pristine shores of Garrison Reach north of Bismarck, an area that retains its pre-settlement look and feel.*

with both hands, he filled me in on the area's history and prehistory. We turned off on a rutted dirt road, then hiked to the top of a tall bluff for a view. It was magnificent—a sweeping vista of the Missouri where it makes a huge loop and of the pleated hills, furry with dun-colored grasses beyond.

"This area has always been very sacred to the tribe," Sheldon said. "There's a prehistoric earth lodge site discovered by the U.S. Army Corps of Engineers. Of course, we can't say exactly where it is."

The view alone is enough to make the place holy. The river takes a nearly 30-mile bend here, and you can see the huge bulge of land formed by the curve, where buffalo and antelope and elk grazed until about 125 years ago. Lewis and Clark (see sidebar, pp. 54-55) brought their Corps of Discovery up

Seven-year-old Selicia Fletcher of the Lower Brule Reservation exemplifies the beauty of Native American ways. Her father, Sheldon (background), a conservation officer, works to protect the reservation and its wildlife.

around this bend in September 1804. Clark wrote: "The bend is a beautiful plain through which I walked, saw numbers of buffalo and goats. . . ." Later, steamboat travelers would disembark on the east side of the Narrows, walk the mile and a half to the west side, and picnic while waiting for the boat to make its slow way around the bend.

Now tremendous circular fields of corn grow on the bulge of land, watered by center-pivot irrigation. The Lower Brule tribe is the main stakeholder in this corporation farm, and popcorn is the principle product, much of it now marketed under the Lakota Foods label. The farm is one of the largest producers of popcorn in the country; it also grows kidney and pinto beans. Yet with no manufacturing and little industry, the tribe desperately needs more economic growth, Sheldon said. Fifty percent unemployment, though low for a reservation, is still too high.

As we hiked down, he pointed out the multitude of plant life: mossy-looking fringe sage, yucca, chokecherry, black currant, buffaloberry, plum trees, red dogwood, kochia (that, when dry, becomes tumbleweed), little prairie sunflowers dancing in the wind, and the ferny yarrow that rabbits and deer love to eat. Last year the Lower Brule tribe reintroduced swift fox and endangered black-footed ferrets onto the reservation as part of an effort to restore biological diversity, and the tribe maintains a herd of 300 buffalo, some of which are harvested for meat.

Limited tourism is one answer to the tribe's problems, Sheldon believes. "We don't want to exploit our culture, but we do want to get some of the benefits of tourism. It's a fine line we have to walk. We'll share this with people if they'll respect it."

Lewis and Clark paused here for a few days, long enough to mingle with the natives and, says Sheldon, for Lewis to father a child who became the grandfather of Sheldon's great-aunt. Clearly proud of both his white and Indian ancestry, Sheldon has the church records to prove it, and he makes a convincing case which he delivers in PowerPoint presentations to historical societies.

"Most of the Lewis and Clark books don't ask about the native point of view," he said. "They don't report the oral histories of native encounters with them."

Along the river here in Lewis and Clark's time, and for several decades afterward, lived Indian chiefs with such names as Iron Nation, Spotted Bull, Split Horn, Clodhopper, Frank Long Horn, and Tight Head. Early maps were marked with these names like towns so that passing traders and travelers would know whom they were dealing with. Sheldon has matched many of the names with historical photographs of

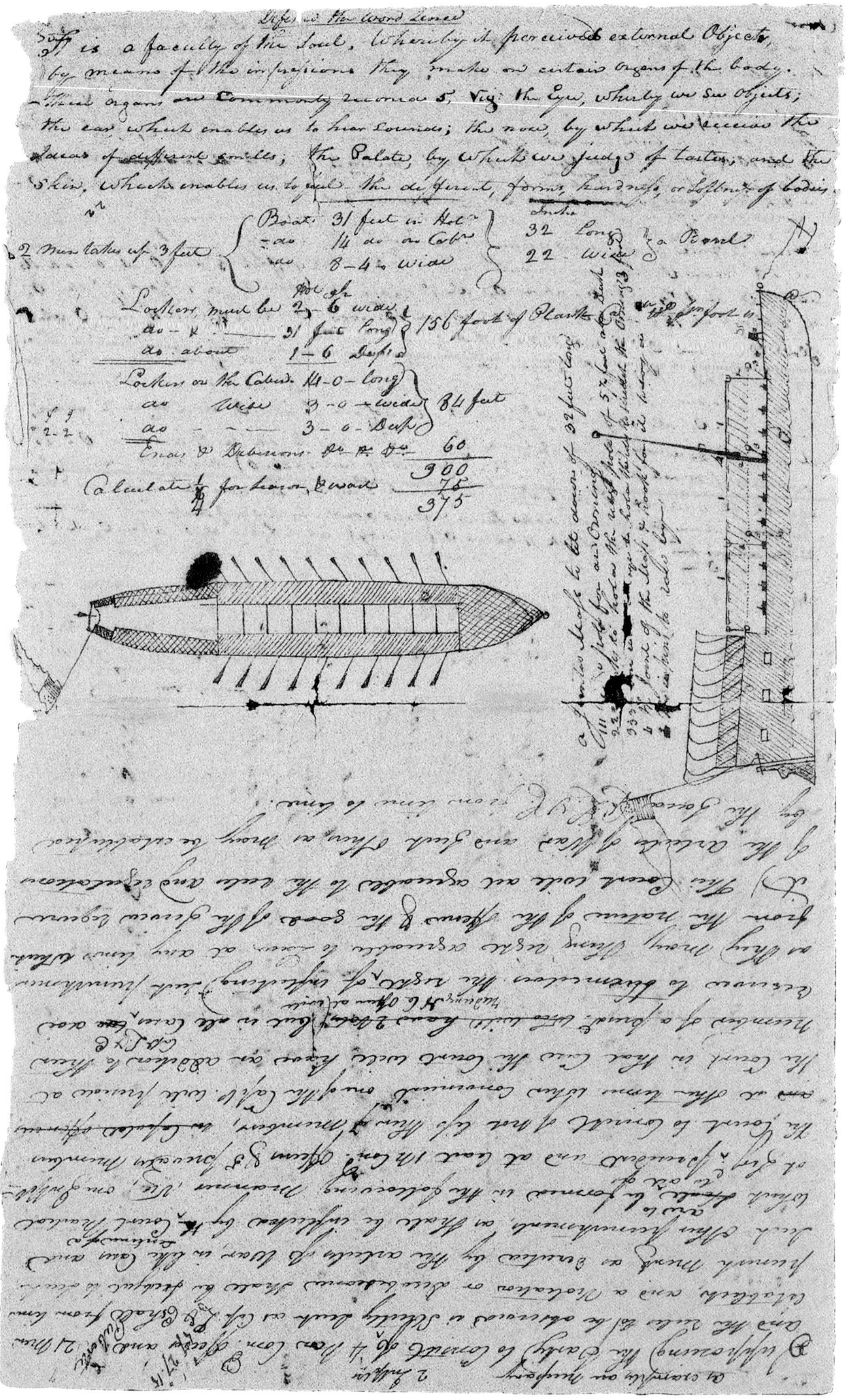

Life is the Word here

Life is a faculty of the soul, whereby it perceives external objects, by means of the impressions they make on certain organs of the body. These organs are commonly reckoned 5, viz; the Eye, whereby we see objects; the ear, which enables us to hear sounds; the nose, by which we receive the ideas of different smells; the Palate, by which we judge of tastes, and the skin, which enables us to feel the different, forms, hardness, or softness of bodies.

Men take up 3 feet

Boat 31 feet in Hol
14 do on Cabin
8–4½ wide

32 Long } a Road
22 Wide

Lockers, must be 2–6 wide
do – 4 31 feet long } 156 feet of Plank
do about 1–6 Depth

Lockers on the Cabin 14–0–long
as Wide 3–0–wide } 84 feet
as 3–0–Depth

Oars & Dubious do do do 60
Calculation for oars & wad 900
75
375

The Boat side are opposite to the side and equidistant from the Bottom of the same & the same, the give equal ... they may they are equidistant ... on our ... number ... the ... examine the light of evening and sunshine ... number of ... ...

the chiefs and hung them in the hall outside his office.

It's true, he says, that the reservations are increasing in population, while many area small towns are staying the same or diminishing. With the unemployment and a majority of the reservation's 1,800 people under age 18, "people have a lot of spare time to get in trouble, whether it's alcohol addiction or drug addiction, and these lead to other things." Suicide and crime rates are notoriously high on South Dakota's reservations. But Sheldon remains optimistic about the future. "If we could get corporate America to look our way, we could turn things around tremendously. We have the resources to do it."

Like many reservations, the Lower Brule has a casino. But unlike the stereotypical Indian casino pulling in millions, this one sits out in the middle of nowhere and competes with casinos nearby. On a weekday morning, a few people—non-Indian—are inside the Golden Buffalo busily pressing buttons amid a warren of blinking, beeping slot machines. At one huge video console an animated dealer periodically asks nobody, "Would you like to play blackjack?" Nearby, a bearded old-timer wearing a jeweler's eyepiece repairs a machine, or perhaps he's rigging it for a slower, or faster, payout. Posted at the door is a notice for a gambler's addiction hotline.

REGIONAL HISTORY 101

LONG BEFORE THE RESERVATIONS AND little towns there were homesteaders, and before them were Lewis and Clark, and before them traders and trappers, and before them the Plains Indians. And before the Plains Indians were the buffalo—streaming, snorting, dust-churning, grass-munching rivers of bison (their proper name)—up to 40 million strong, moving in herds of unimaginable size (picture swarms of bees or flocks of blackbirds), darkening the plain, thundering across the wild open range.

The people who first found their way to this part of the continent some 12,000 years ago made a living hunting the bison. As the buffalo fared, so fared the people (more on this subject in the Plains chapter). They hunted them on foot with spears, disguising themselves in animal hides, or stampeded them off cliffs. Later they used bows and arrows, and with the arrival of horses on European ships, they became experts at hunting on horseback. Living as they did in the middle of the continent, in a place better suited to their nomadic life than the settlers' way, the Plains Indians were the last to yield their lands and lifestyle. First, like

OPPOSITE | *A leaf from William Clark's notebook shows the keelboat designed by Meriwether Lewis; the 55-foot-long boat could hold 12 tons.*

Down and out in Pierre, South Dakota: Farmers driven from their land by drought line up for a 1936 Works Progress Administration job, construction of a dam at nearby Lake Arikara that will help conserve precious water.

advance artillery, came smallpox and other diseases, moving up the river with devastating sureness in the late 1700s and early 1800s, decimating one tribe after another. Then came the settlers themselves.

The Missouri was the avenue into the Dakota territory, and it was to bring a steady army of ranchers, farmers, and miners. The actual U.S. Army began operations here during the 1860s with attempts to build roads into the gold fields of Wyoming; territorial battles with the Sioux followed. During the next two decades, gold was discovered in

South Dakota's Black Hills (see the Black Hills chapter), old treaties were violated, and the railroad brought endless cars of hunters and settlers. The Indians had to give up hunting the buffalo, which had nearly been exterminated, and settle onto reservations. In 1889 North Dakota and South Dakota became the 39th and 40th states to enter the Union.

The 20th century was marked by a boom-and-bust economy, periods of prosperity and hardship following one after the other. The worst years for the Dakotas, like the rest of middle America, were the 1930s—a decade of

A dash of opulence on the prairie, the South Dakota state capitol in Pierre takes on the amber tones of sunset. Completed in 1910, the fieldstone, limestone, and marble building stands 161 feet high.

severe drought, accompanied by dust storms that literally wiped away many farms. Some 6 percent of the population of North and South Dakota, or about 89,000 people, left. It took half a century for the population of South Dakota to recover; the population of North Dakota has never again reached its 1930 high of 681,000.

After much wrangling, the capital of South Dakota was chosen for its location in the approximate center of the state. Today Pierre (pronounced "peer") ranks as the second smallest state capital (after Montpelier), with a population of 14,000. Situated on the east side of the Missouri River, the "city" was named for explorer Pierre Gaultier de Varennes, whose French-Canadian sons were the first known non-Indians to enter what is now South Dakota. In 1743 they buried an inscribed lead plate across the river at present-day Fort Pierre. Three teenagers found the plate in 1913, and you can see it in the South Dakota Cultural Heritage Center.

FOLLOWING PAGES | *Sunflowers face the morning sun on the Standing Rock Indian Reservation, just south of Fort Yates, North Dakota.*

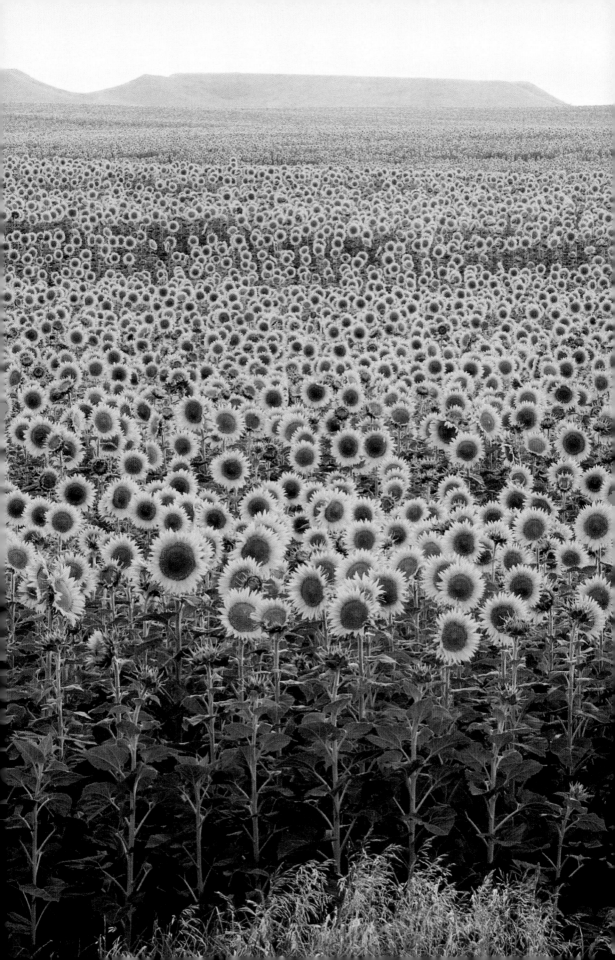

Pierre holds a number of surprises, starting with the capitol itself. Its grandeur is like nothing else for hundreds of miles. The columned portico leads to an opulent rotunda soaring 96 feet. Stained-glass skylights, glass-and-terrazzo floors, 19th-century paintings, and marble stairways lend a palatial air. Outside, beautifully maintained grounds form a park, and an adjacent lake is set off by memorial statuary—the whole peaceful and lovely and nearly deserted when I visited. Bikers and dog walkers take to a path by the river, where Lewis and Clark trail signage dates from the recent bicentennial hoopla.

North of the capitol, the Cultural Heritage Center is bermed into a hill-

Cattails grow along the Missouri River near Fort Pierre, South Dakota. Lewis and Clark held council here with the Teton Sioux; the Indians attempted to take the explorers' pirogue and its cargo.

side like a homesteader's dugout. Among the treasures inside are a Medora-to-Deadwood stagecoach and film clips from the 1930s drought. Yet the Indian objects—with their alternate reality, their peephole into a South Dakota that might have been and then suddenly was no more—have the most imagination-sparking power. Whose were the last feet to wear that pair of late-1800s moccasins? Was she dancing by a flickering fire, a wooden flute playing softly in the dark? That steel-pointed arrow—what was it like to shoot it at a buffalo? an enemy? to have it stuck in your side? Here hangs a Ghost Dance shirt removed from the body of a Mniconju man killed at Wounded Knee in 1890 (wearers believed such shirts would protect them from the white man's bullets). It's a fringed white muslin shirt, an eagle feather attached to each sleeve—nothing elaborate, yet its ghostly pallor, its tale of hope and loss, is almost unbearably sad. The massacre at Wounded Knee was the terrible, final showdown in the whites versus Indians drama. Nearby is a buffalo skull owned by Chief Sitting Bull; it was placed on a medicine pole during Ghost Dances at the Standing Rock Reservation. Some tribal elders think such relics are too sacred for display.

Across the river at Fort Pierre, where the Bad River joins the Missouri, Lewis and Clark held council in September 1804 with the Teton Sioux, followed by feasting and celebration that Clark described as a "tense three days." It marked the first meeting of United States officials and the Sioux nation. Today the little down-at-the-heels town of Fort Pierre has a one-block downtown featuring the usual steakhouse and saloons in early 1900s buildings as well as a bank, clothing store, saddle shop, taxidermy shop, paperback shop, and exotic dancing club.

Motel owner Mike Schwinier says the area is big with hunters and fishermen. Walleye is king around here, and varmint hunting ("really just shooting," he says) is so popular that there is an annual championship. Varmints get no peace. It's open season and no limits on prairie dogs and coyotes, both considered pests to ranchers—the prairie dogs for eating grass and the coyotes for poaching livestock. And when you tire of hunting you can always take a drive. "Just for something to do, I like to get on my motorbike and ride about 30 miles through the reservation at around sunset. You have to watch out for the deer." The highway along the river is a wonderful stretch of open American road, the landscape nearly untouched by human hand.

North from Pierre, on a long, arrow-straight road, colorful fields of sunflowers carpet the roadsides, as well as milo, wheat, alfalfa, and barley,

Friday night lights in Wilton, North Dakota: High-school football players watch a game under a cloud-filled sky. With low student populations, many area schools field 9-man teams instead of the standard 11.

stretching into the far distance. Big planted fields alternate with fallow fields. A lone tree on a rise seems remarkable. A barn, house, and silo mark the only habitation for miles and miles. Occasionally a pickup truck passes, driven by a man or woman wearing a cowboy hat.

NORTH TO LAKE SAKAKAWEA

ABOUT 110 MILES NORTH, THE LITTLE town of Mobridge was named for the simple presence of a bridge across the river. Just outside of town a monument to Sitting Bull marks his gravesite on an appealing bluff above the river.

"He's not buried there," William Brave Bull told me, "but the town of Mobridge will never admit to it. The publicity is too good." A recent graduate of the Institute of American Indian Arts in Santa Fe, New Mexico, William is a soft-spoken, unassuming young man with long, straight black hair and a serious but friendly demeanor. He now lives in the Standing Rock Reservation, which spills across the border of North Dakota. He works with his mother's tourism company

Banner and smile at the ready, a flag bearer gets set to march in the River City Band Festival in Chamberlain, South Dakota, an annual competition bringing together some 20 area high school bands.

and does consulting and acting for documentaries. William explains that Sitting Bull was buried in a mass grave and that robbers came and took the first bones they happened upon, claiming they were Sitting Bull's. He points me to the real, unspectacular burial site, up the road in the little reservation town of Fort Yates. There a marker states, "He was buried here but his grave has been vandalized many times. This marker is directly over the gravesite." Little stones placed on the marker by visitors indicate that to most people this is indeed the spot.

William's comments on the future of the reservation echoed Sheldon's. "We have a good shot at bringing more tourism here," he said. "But the tribe has got to take a more active role in protecting the sacred sites." He was especially concerned that access to such ceremonies as the Sun Dance be off limits to the merely curious.

Down at the river a Lewis and Clark sign has been vandalized, but the words are still legible: On October 15, 1804, the expedition paused near Fort Yates and traded with 30 Arikaras. Lewis noted, "Those people were kind and appeared to be much pleased with the attention we paid them." One has to wonder at the motive behind the vandalism. The rest of Fort Yates is mostly a dreary clutch of squat one-story houses, a couple of stores, some tribal buildings, and a Taco John's eatery. It's as if the town were saying, *Look at the land if you're looking for beauty, not at what man makes.*

Not far upriver, the capital of North Dakota started out, like many cities in the region, as a fort. The town that grew up here was named in 1873 for German chancellor Otto von Bismarck as an incentive for Germans to invest in the local railroad. Bismarck then went on to prosper as a rail center, gold mine outfitter, and general frontier boomtown; it became the territorial capital in 1883 and the state capital six years later. In addition to being the seat of state government, the city now serves as a shipping headquarters for the region's ranch, farm, and mine products. With a population of 56,000, Bismarck ranks as second largest city in the western Dakotas (after Rapid City, South Dakota).

Sharp outfits and on-pitch music make for a winning combination at Chamberlain's River City Band Festival, a cultural highlight in this South Dakota town, whose population holds steady at about 2,300.

Recalling bygone days, a rendezvous at Fort Union Trading Post National Historic Site keeps history alive. Established on the Missouri River in 1828, the post soon became a nexus of trappers, Indians, and pioneers.

When novelist John Steinbeck passed through while researching his 1962 classic, *Travels with Charley*, he was amazed at the difference in landscape from one side of the river to the other. Crossing from Bismarck to the west side he was suddenly in western America, "with brown grass and water scorings and small outcrops. The two sides of the river might well be a thousand miles apart." Of course, if he had been travel-ing along the river instead of just cross-ing it, he would have seen that same dif-ference everywhere.

The capitol grounds sparkle on a crisp morning, lushly groomed greenswards and plantings creating a northern plains oasis. The 19-story capitol building springs from this focal point, its height and deco contours an anomaly among capitols and among anything in this part of the country—from various places in the city you can see the "skyscraper of the prairie" towering above everything else.

Next door to the capitol, the North Dakota Heritage Center displays a number of interesting historical objects. The skull of an ancestral buffalo, Bison latifrons, is a revelation. Found not far northwest, on the Fort Berthold Reservation, the 47,500-year-old skull measures six feet from the tip of one horn to the other. Modern bison look plenty big; these Ice Age beasts were half again as large. Another display case shows not one but four painted Ghost Dance shirts, one of them supposedly owned by Sitting Bull, though it is said he never wore one. One thing he did wear seems particularly noble in Sioux fashion—a necklace adorned with carved

Popcorn is a major crop on the Lower Brule and other places along the Missouri.

deer hooves, brass bells, and eagle and hawk claws. Nearby, a handwritten order from Standing Rock agent James McLaughlin authorizes the immediate arrest of Sitting Bull on December 14, 1890: "PS. You must not let him escape under any circumstances."

Across the river from Bismarck lies Fort Abraham Lincoln State Park, which presents an interesting combination of

both Native American and U.S. Army history. The story begins about A.D. 900, when the tribal groups that later formed the Mandans arrived in the Dakotas. The Mandans themselves established several villages near here, including On-a-Slant, which thrived from about 1575 to 1781. But then a smallpox epidemic swept through, and the Mandans moved about 70 miles upriver, joining with the Arikara. When Lewis and Clark came by in 1804 they camped near the ruins of the villages, but there were no Indians.

Skip to 1872, when Fort Abraham Lincoln was established on a bluff above the old village site to protect frontier settlers and railroad surveyors. One of the fort's first commanding officers was Gen. George A. Custer, who embarked from here in May 1876 for his fateful skirmish with the Sioux and Cheyenne at the Little Bighorn in Montana. Today the reconstructed fort holds a granary, commissary, enlisted men's barracks, and, most interesting of all, a re-creation of the Commanding

FOLLOWING PAGES | *Morning shadows of autumn-yellow cottonwoods and hay bales brush long strokes on fields near the Garrison Dam.*

CROSS RANCH STATE PARK

Though the Missouri in the Dakotas is hardly what one would call "developed," some places take one way back into primitive times. Such a place is found at Cross Ranch and its adjoining preserve. The 589-acre park and 6,000-acre Nature Conservancy preserve occupy part of what was once an 11,000-acre ranch owned in the late 1800s by A.D. Gaines, professor of classical literature and land agent for the Northern Pacific Railroad. These pristine parcels make up the largest tract of publicly owned floodplain forest on this part of the Missouri.

Called the Garrison Reach, the 60 or so miles of river below the Garrison Dam encompass the longest stretch of free-flowing Missouri River from here all the way down to St. Louis. True, the dam prevents the river from flooding and thus alters the old cycle of forest succession. But the river retains more or less its original contours all along this stretch, and Cross Ranch is just about the best place to see it.

Trails looping through the riparian woodlands and edging the river take hikers into a time warp: Giant cottonwoods rustle in the wind like the sound of rain, while from 20-foot banks you can see the muddy Missouri lapping the shore and sliding by. Terns and piping plovers alight on sandbars across the sun-spangled water. A muskrat noses along the shore, then ducks under; overhead a hawk circles in search of prey.

Another trail winds through a piece of prairie where a homestead was built in 1882; the foundations are still visible. Native grasses cover the low hills here—bluestem, grama, wheat grass, and needle grass move in the wind as if stroked by an unseen hand. Wildflowers and prairie birds like the nighthawk and western meadowlark add splashes of vibrant color to the scene. On a separate parcel to the south grow some of the largest cottonwoods in the state. Up to 300 years old, these trees measure more than 15 feet in circumference and 100 feet in height.

Officer's Headquarters, which Custer and his wife, Libbie, occupied during their stay here. Appearing much as it did in the 1870s, the prairie house has a sweeping front porch and a cellar like the one where Custer kept his pet bobcat. Over in the reconstructed On-a-Slant village, where some 1,500 people once lived, I took a look inside an earth lodge—it was dark and dank, but a fire would've been going in Mandan days.

Thirty miles north of Bismarck as the crow flies, but well over an hour on a network of increasingly small roads, lies Cross Ranch State Park, about as pristine a patch of Missouri bottom-land as survives (see sidebar, p. 43). The completion of Garrison Dam in 1956 some 50 miles upstream is slowly alter-ing the local ecology: Without periodic flooding, for instance, the cottonwoods are giving way to green ash and bur oak. But bald eagles and deer still haunt the woods, and migrating geese, terns, and whooping cranes still gather on the river's sandbars. It was at Cross Ranch that I encountered an unusual man named Chip Cartwright.

NORTH DAKOTA BLACK HISTORY

ONE OF THE FEW BLACK PARK RANGERS IN the West, Cartwright grew up in segregat-ed Virginia, sharing an 800-square-foot home with his parents and six siblings. He used to play in the old earthworks around Petersburg, throwing "rocks" that he later discovered were Civil War minie balls. After a military stint, he entered the forest service, became its first black ranger, and spent the bulk of his career as a forester in various locations around the country. He retired a couple of years ago and began traveling, ending up in the home state of his ex-wife. Looking into the local history, he became intrigued by York, William Clark's slave, who was a vital member of the Lewis and Clark expedition. "When I found out he was from near where I was from, I thought it was a natural."

Cartwright did more research and developed a presentation about York's life and contributions; he began giving it at Fort Mandan, a few miles north of Cross Ranch. When asked to take on a job as a seasonal interpreter at Cross Ranch, he accepted. "I discovered I was not only an interpreter of nature, but a storyteller."

In addition to presenting York, Cartwright also does programs on buf-falo soldiers (black soldiers of the Old West) and black cowboys. Of some 36,000 total cowboys in the open-range days, fully 25 percent were black, accord-ing to Cartwright. "On some trail drives, only the boss was white." For his presen-tations, he dresses the part, interpreting York's life in the third person and fic-tional characters in the first. He stresses that his stories all come from docu-mented facts. What he could not find specifically about York, for example, he was able to infer from records of slavery in Virginia. His buffalo soldier is an escaped slave who volunteers for the cavalry as a way of obtaining his freedom and proving to white society at large that he is worthy of being free. Though Cartwright does not see many black tourists, he gets a large number of people who are surprised and interested that North Dakota has a black history. "Many folks don't know that the first non-

Indian baby born in the North Dakota territory was born to a black slave."

Cartwright RVs in the off-season, but keeps returning to North Dakota for its people and its open spaces: "I like the farming ethic here. And there's something about being on these windswept prairie lands—you can see forever." It's the natural world that first attracted him to forestry, and when he's in his ranger uniform he's all about nature. After our visit, he was heading off to lead a walk

At a rollicking Lewis and Clark Days dance, couples whirl and glide under the streetlights of Washburn, North Dakota. The recent revival of interest in the explorers has helped bolster the area's economy.

with a busload of sixth graders. "Today my message is about nature. I want them to understand that what you do today, the choices you make, can affect the future."

Not far north of Cross Ranch, the town of Washburn occupies a bluff on the Missouri, an ideal site for riverboat trade in the late 1800s. Two later arteries—the railroad and U.S. route 83—have kept the town alive into the 21st century. A bridge on the edge of town crosses the Missouri and leads back two centuries. Sandbars may have shifted over the years, but the tree-lined shores remain as undeveloped in this area of long winters as what Lewis and Clark saw—in fact, with the Indians gone, the shores are probably even less developed.

A blade from the Knife River Indian Villages originated in England.

Despite the severity of those winters, Indians for centuries occupied a number of sites along the river west of Wash-burn. One key village area sits above the Knife River, just before its confluence with the Missouri. The Knife River Indian Villages, now a national historic site, shows evidence of occupation for more than 11,000 years. More than 50 depressions in the ground mark where earth lodges once

stood. Measuring 30 to 60 feet in diameter, these lodges housed up to 15 people, their belongings, and dogs. A framework of wood rafters and support posts was roofed with a five-inch layer of earth.

Some 400 Hidatsa people lived here from the 1790s to the 1830s in a village called Awatixa (ah-wah-TEE-khah), intermarrying at times with Mandan to the south. They traveled the river in circular bullboats (made by stretching a hide over a framework of willows), which carried dried meat downriver from hunts. Women built and navigated them; Lewis and Clark found them almost impossible to maneuver. Among part-time Awatixa residents was a French-Canadian trader named Toussaint Char-bonneau and his Sho-shone wife, Sacagawea. Lewis and Clark hired them as translators and they left with the Corps in April 1805.

OPPOSITE | *Dimples along the banks of the Knife River in North Dakota mark the site of Awatixa village, where Sacagawea once lived.*
FOLLOWING PAGES | *At Fort Union Trading Post National Historic Site, west of Williston, North Dakota, a teepee stands sentinel.*

Later visitors included American artist George Catlin and Swiss artist Karl Bodmer; their colorful paintings provide an invaluable record of village life. Wrote Catlin: "I loved a people who have always made me welcome to the best they had—who are honest without laws . . . who worship God without a Bible . . . who never fought a battle with the white man except on their own ground."

In 1835 a Sioux raiding party burned the village. A few years later, a smallpox epidemic forced the remaining Hidatsa and Mandan, joined by the Arikara, farther upriver. In 1885 the U.S. government ordered the three tribes to occupy the Fort Berthold Reservation, where they remain today.

In addition to the circular depressions, the site features a reconstructed earth lodge—an original one could not exist since they only lasted about ten years. A buffalo robe at the entry keeps the cold out; inside, the fireplace is centrally located on the hard earth floor, while an opening in the roof vents smoke. One can imagine the wind roaring across the plains and fluting like mournful spirits around the smoke hole.

FORTS AT THE CONFLUENCE

TO THE NORTH, THE RIVER SUDDENLY balloons into Lake Sakakawea, a 200-mile-long swelling created by the Garrison Dam. You can drive across the 2.5-mile-long dam, one of the largest earthen dams in the world. It stands 210 feet high (almost as high as the capitol in Bismarck) and measures 60 feet wide at the top. The dam protects downstream states from flooding and provides water for irrigation, navigation, and electricity.

To the west and north, the Fort Berthold Reservation spreads for 450,000 acres on both sides of the lake. Reduced to about one-third of its original size, the reservation was then partially flooded by the creation of the lake. Cattle and horses graze the wide pastures of this ruggedly beautiful land. In the northwest corner of the reservation stands the Four Bears Casino and a hamlet called New Town, built when the town of Sanish was flooded by the lake.

Right near the border of Montana, Fort Union dates from 1828. Not a military fort, it was an outpost of John Jacob Astor's far-reaching American Fur Company. A frontier shopping mall, the trading post once buzzed with Indian and white trappers and traders exchanging beaver pelts and buffalo hides for knives, muskets, powder, steel traps, clothes, glass beads, sugar, coffee, and liquor. Steamboats, keelboats, and disposable mackinaws plied the river, ferrying goods up and down. Up to 100 people lived in

OPPOSITE | *Like an ancestral spirit, smoke rises to the vent of prayer man Arlie Knight's earth lodge on the Fort Berthold Reservation in North Dakota.*

LEWIS AND CLARK

In May 1804 a military expedition of 45 men under the command of Meriwether Lewis and William Clark set out from St. Louis for points west. Their job was to find a water route to the Pacific (if such existed), and along the way to catalogue the plants, animals, minerals, landforms, and native peoples. They were to head up the Missouri River, cross the Rocky Mountains, and travel into the disputed Northwest Territory. Most of the trip was a matter of following the river upstream, and until they came to what is now central North Dakota they traced a route fairly well-known to earlier explorers and traders. But after this they were plunging into territory new to Europeans.

The entire trip was a chronicle of one exciting, dangerous adventure after another, and the Dakotas portion was to hold some of the most interesting episodes. Heading upriver through South Dakota in a keelboat and pirogues, the crew passed the spectacular Big Bend area and continued north, encountering Indian tribes all along the way. They spent their first winter near some Mandan villages just west of present-day Washburn, North Dakota. It took them six weeks to build a 1,600-square-foot shelter, which they called Fort Mandan. Despite the brutally cold winter, the crew apparently got along well together and enjoyed friendly, even intimate, relations with the Mandan, partaking happily in their games, music, dances, food, and lovely women.

Twice that winter Sioux raiders made attacks—once against Mandan hunters and once against a group of white crewmen. A Mandan was killed and many horses were stolen. Lewis and 24 men trekked 30 miles out into deep snow looking for the marauders, but finally gave up, instead turning the chase into a hunting party and bringing back 2,400 pounds of meat. Clark's assessment of the Teton Sioux was a prophecy of the coming conflict between settlers and Sioux: "These are the vilest miscreants of the savage race. Unless these people are reduced to order by coercive measures, I am ready to pronounce that the citizens of the United States can never enjoy but partially the advantages which the Missouri presents."

The winter camp was also notable for the signing on of three new crew members. Lewis and Clark hired French-Canadian trader Toussaint Charbonneau, who was living with the Mandan, as a translator. His wife, Sacagawea, was a Shoshone girl of about 17, who had been kidnapped several years earlier by the Hidatsa. In February

Meriwether Lewis (1774-1809, right) invited his frontier militia leader, William Clark, (1770-1838, left) to co-command an expedition of discovery across two-thirds of the continent.

1805 she gave birth to Jean Baptiste. Charbonneau signed his family on for the expedition but said he did not want to do any heavy work or stand guard, and he wanted to be able to leave when he felt like it. Lewis and Clark would not agree to these terms, and a week later Charbonneau accepted their original offer. Both Charbonneau and Sacagawea would prove invaluable with Indian languages up the trail, and the disarming presence of a teenager and her baby was often a diplomatic icebreaker. The little family stayed with the crew until their return to Fort Mandan in August 1806. Indians in North Dakota continue to bear the surname Charbonneau to this day.

Lewis and Clark signs and centers are now strung along the Missouri's bordering roads like beads on a strand, many of them placed during the 2004-06 bicentennial.

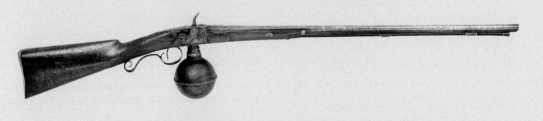

Lewis's air gun was fueled by compressed air instead of powder, a single canister powering 40 sparkless shots. Its value as a weapon aside, the gun impressed Indians with its "majic."
OPPOSITE | *William Clark carried this pocket compass on the 1804-06 expedition.*

the fort at one time. Among famous visitors were painters George Catlin, Karl Bodmer, and John James Audubon. Waves of smallpox traveling upriver and the encroachment of white civilization brought the post's days to an end by 1867. Troops from nearby Fort Buford tore it down and hauled away the remains.

Today the fort has been reconstructed, tepees sitting outside the stockade, just as they would have in summers past. Beyond a grassy field runs the railroad, in juxtaposition to the fort's historical milieu, when the river was the highway. Inside the stockade, the elaborate two-story bourgeois' (manager's) house, brightly trimmed in red, blue, and green, looks as spiffy as a vacation cottage in Cape May.

Here I met ranger Loren Yellow Bird. Of Arikara and Hidatsa descent, he grew up on the Fort Berthold reservation and has worked in a number of national parks. He tries to give a balance to the stories told at Fort Union. "There's not a lot of documentation from the native point of view," he told me. "And what there is is not always understood." Trained in anthropology, he never thought of himself as a historian until coming here seven years ago. "It's interesting listening to people come here with certain ideas and preconceptions. I try to correct them. People will ask how many soldiers were here, or they say, 'Well, they were safe here where the

Indians couldn't get them.' They don't realize that the purpose of the fort was to trade with the Indians."

A few miles away, the Yellowstone River joins with the Missouri. The reason there is no city at this major confluence is that the U.S. Army constructed Fort Buford here in 1866 and established a 30-square-mile military reservation, off-limits to settlers. A state historic site, the fort is best known as the surrender location of Sitting Bull in 1881. Said the Sioux chief, "I wish it to be remembered that I was the last man in my tribe to surrender my rifle." The parade ground is now a honey-colored grassy plain.

As for the confluence, it remains about as untouched as it was when Lewis and Clark saw it. They beheld immense numbers of antelope, beaver, elk, deer, buffalo, ducks, geese, and eagles. While the wildlife is no longer as abundant, the bottomland is still lined with cottonwoods, elms, and oaks, with not a building in sight. Clark measured the rivers and found the Yellowstone wider at 858 yards from bank to bank; the Missouri was 520. The Yellowstone is today the longest undammed river in the contiguous United States. The two rivers continue on into the mountains of Montana, while we turn our attention to the Dakota plains.

OPPOSITE | *Fall bedecks hills along the Missouri River near Bismarck. For most of its journey through the Dakotas, the river traverses wild or rural lands.*

CHAPTER TWO

PLAINS

THE WIDE AND ROLLING PRAIRIE

ith the exception of the Black Hills, the Dakotas west of the Missouri almost all fall within the Northern Great Plains. The area is sometimes referred to by its most distinguishing feature, the Badlands, though those heavily eroded places actually occupy only parts of the western Dakotas. This chapter, then, takes a look at all that vast in-between space—the places that are not the river, the Badlands, or the Black Hills. It's a lot of space. What's in it? Grass, for one thing. Acres and acres and acres of barely rolling ranches where cattle and horses and sometimes sheep or buffalo graze on short and mixed-grass ranges, farms planted to hay and wheat and sorghum, and national grasslands where native prairie grasses grow as wild as they did before the coming of settlers.

A flag found after the June 1876 Battle of Little Bighorn, in which George Custer died.
OPPOSITE | *Prairie grasses glisten at sunrise in the Little Missouri National Grassland near Medora, North Dakota.* **PREVIOUS PAGES** | *Roundup for branding time on the ranch of Gary Jepson in Killdeer, North Dakota.*

Keeping old traditions alive, a Corpus Christi procession blends elements of formality and informality at the 1887 Saint Clements Catholic Church north of Glen Ullin, North Dakota.

YOU CAN DRIVE FOR MILES AND MILES through such scenery and never be bored—there is always a sense of something getting ready to happen. On the horizon a butte suddenly rises a thousand feet above the plain; steel gray clouds in the distance portend rain; the rain comes and in the mist afterward a tremendous heart-filling rainbow arcs across a quarter of the entire sky. The sky itself seems limitless, larger than the largest ocean you have ever seen. You cannot help looking to the sky for drama, and in doing so you often find your spirits lifting off, your sense of permanence becoming unmoored. "The beauty of the plains," wrote Ian Frazier in Great Plains, "is not just in themselves but in the sky, in what you think when you look at them, and in what they are not."

There are also small towns with little museums and saloons, Indian reservations, oil rigs, abandoned houses and churches out in the middle of nowhere, towns that are little more than a gas station and a granary. And there are of course the people who occupy these places, though you could drive all day and imagine that the towns were movie

Sunset on a country church: Tombstone-like arches of golden light rise beneath broken rafters in Glucksdahl Lutheran Church; services were last held in this Bentley, North Dakota, building in 1955.

sets or that the world had ended but that country music was somehow still being broadcast.

HOMESTEADERS AND FLINT KNAPPERS

AT 70 MILES PER HOUR—WHAT MOST people do on the backroads—the miles go by quickly, and you can suddenly find yourself in a place like the Buffalo Gap National Grassland. The national grasslands were established in 1960 to help regenerate the native grasses that had been destroyed during the Dust Bowl of the 1930s. The settlers who poured into the area in the late 1800s and early 1900s had no idea that plowing up the land would eventually lead to disaster. A finely tuned ecosystem that had developed over millennia—the perfect mix of grasses on the perfect kind of soil, with just the right amount of rainfall—was suddenly changed. The sages and grasses that had adapted to the grazing of buffalo, the digging of prairie dogs, and the occasional prairie fires were uprooted and replaced with crops. A prolonged drought in the 1930s dried up the topsoil and the region's incessant winds carried it away—in

Wildflowers grow in the Little Missouri National Grasslands, North Dakota. Encompassing 503,000 acres, the Little Missouri, like the other Dakotas grasslands, is helping restore a native prairie ecosystem.

clouds rising up to 20,000 feet. The dust buried whole farms—fences, roads, and all—piling in drifts ten feet deep; it blew in storms all the way to the East Coast and settled on the President's desk in Washington, D.C. Coinciding with the Great Depression years, the Dust Bowl drove tens of thousands of people from the Dakotas. Franklin Roosevelt's recovery and emergency acts were the first steps taken by the government to purchase and restore the ruined lands.

Five of the country's 20 national grasslands lie in the western Dakotas. The largest in the country, the Little Missouri, is in North Dakota; the Grand River and Cedar River National Grassland straddles the border; the Fort Pierre lies just south of Pierre; and the Buffalo Gap spreads in right-angled lots across southwestern South Dakota. Altogether, these units make up about 1.4 million acres of grasslands, on which the native grasses have come back in rich variety. Among nearly 40 species of native grass are western wheat grass, big bluestem, needle-and-thread, buffalo grass, and sideoats grama. Since these are public lands, you can hike on them anywhere you like; you can also hunt, fish, bike, pitch a tent, drive an ATV, and even pick up fossils, as long as they're invertebrate and you don't dig for them.

I was content to find a piece of prairie far off the main roads and just start walking. What appeared from the road to be flat and monotonous was vivid and alive. Prairie dog holes dotted patches of bare ground, around which were prickly pear cactus with fleshy red fruits. Beyond, in the buffalo grass,

came the kill-dee-dee-dee of invisible killdeer. Geese flew up from a water hole. The colors were soft and subtle, and beyond the rustlings of birds and insects a huge stillness filled the land.

A 1930 poem, "Prayer of the Homesteader," lays out the frustration

FOLLOWING PAGES | *A prophetic sky gathers over the plains surrounding U.S. Highway 212 west of Eagle Butte, South Dakota.*

Horses graze in the Grand River and Cedar River National Grassland near Bison, South Dakota. This 155,000-acre parcel of rolling hills and river banks is carpeted with drought-resistant mixed-grass prairie.

of early farmers: "Lord, can it be that this is not your land? Your ways are peaceful ways through country lanes. But you have never walked these plains, we never see your face beneath these skies. . . . This land fights. Its hard brown sod protests against the plow, its stubborn grasses cling. . . . Lord, did you mean that men should farm this land?"

The short answer is a resounding No. Instead of farming, most plains people now ranch, and at 20 acres to sustain a single cow, the average ranch size is 5,000 acres. Low-moisture-requiring crops such as sorghum and sunflowers (grown for oil) do okay in the western Dakotas, but not much else. The Northern Plains are high and dry—at 2,000 to 3,000 feet above sea level, not quite as high as the High Plains to the south, but still high. The region receives about 17 inches of rainfall a year (New York City gets 50).

The Homestead Act of 1862 offered 160 acres of land to anyone who would

Angels guard an old iron-cross cemetery near Killdeer, North Dakota. Iron crosses marked the graves of many Ukrainian and Russian immigrants to the area in the early 1900s.

pay a small filing fee, improve the land, and live on it most of the year for five straight years. The good land lay along the few valleys and had already been given to the railroads; the remains were pieces of wind-whipped grassland that sounded like Elysian fields to eager young farmers in Germany, Norway, Ireland, and England. They built homes in the sides of hills, or freestanding, with what little wood they could find, covered by two-foot-long strips of sod. The sodbusters began pouring in like the wind itself, sure that the rain would follow the plow, just as the promotional literature promised. It didn't, and they either gutted it out or left.

Long before the settlers arrived, native people lived on the Dakota plains. One place they kept returning to for some 11,000 years lies along the Knife River near the tiny town of Dunn Center, North Dakota. The farmer who bought the place in 1948 decided to raise cattle instead of crops when he found his field was pocked with little craters. His son and daughter-in-law, Allan and Gail Lynch, discovered in 1968 that what Allan's father had thought might be buffalo wallows were in fact little flint quarries. Archaeologists have determined that many of the 2,500 depressions were dug by Indians as far back as 11,200 years ago for the local flint, which they knapped into arrowheads, knives, and

other tools that could be used as barter items in a large trade network across the Great Plains.

Gail showed me around the site one crisp clear morning. Allan has placed fence posts where he discovered anvil stones, which he has left in situ. The whole site sits unassumingly on a green pasture, the ten-foot-wide shallow pits grown over with grass and sage. Black Angus cows with green ear tags stood watching as Gail demonstrated how the natives would take an anvil stone and peck away at a grayish rock, flaking off pieces of sharp-edged, translucent, root-beer-colored flint. "This is one of the best kept secrets in North Dakota," she told me. "It's probably one of the largest flint quarries in the United States." She said that Indians from various parts of the country have come here and told her they can feel that it is sacred ground, that no fighting was done here: "There were good spirits here; otherwise, they said, we wouldn't be able to live here." The last time the area was quarried, Gail told me, was just over 200 years ago. Altogether, perhaps 67 tons of flint were removed from the site over the millennia—that's about a million cubic feet, or enough to make 160 million tools.

Several such quarry sites exist in Dunn County and neighboring Mercer County, but the Lynch site—covering half a square mile—has the highest concentration of quarry pits. It's what

Ready for the judges, a goat and its owner hope to pocket prizes at the Butte-Lawrence County Fair in Nisland, South Dakota, one of many such events displaying the best of the western Dakotas' rural economy.

Allan calls the "mother lode" of the area. His grandfather came to Dunn County as a homesteader in 1908; Allan's father then had to sell out 40 years later when the creation of Lake Sakakawea flooded the north part of the county. He bought this ranch and leased it to a coal company; the lease expires in 2011. "We're just crossing our fingers that they won't mine here," Allan says. "That's why we're fighting so hard to get this designated as a national historical landmark." Every year he and Gail take 100 or more people out to the site—in groups or singly—without charge. Though there is no advertising, people find out about it and come—amateur flint knappers and archaeology buffs are especially interested.

The Lynches have done very well in the local oil business, profiting from a recent boom similar to ones that have occurred in these parts for the last 50 years. For the past two years new wells have been dug and pipelines laid at a tremendous pace. As a contract pumper, Allan's job is to inspect oil rigs for Conoco Phillips and other companies, make sure everything is in working order, and call in roustabouts when something needs attention. Gail points to a new well being drilled on a distant hill. "Things are really hopping," she says. "There's major, major things going on. It's just crazy."

Prodigy in the saddle: A young wrangler flashes hardware earned at the annual Youth Rodeo in Bowman, North Dakota, where youngsters 14 and under compete for prizes in cowboy skills.

It seems everywhere I go in the northwest part of the state, there are rigs, sitting like giant mosquitoes, constantly siphoning oil from deep in the ground. On this landscape oil tanks are as common as grain silos. The focal point of the activity, Williston (population a mere 12,500) has 600 motel beds, yet not one to be found on a normal weekday. The answer: "Just regular business—oilmen." With new technology, drillers can explore horizontally, not just vertically, in search of oil pools. The Bakken shale formation, a layer only 5 to 20 feet thick, lies 2 miles beneath the earth's surface. Once the rig drills into this formation, it can be steered horizontally another mile to find the oil. Some estimates claim the region contains 400 billion barrels of oil—more than the Arctic National Wildlife Refuge—and that the high price of oil will only continue and thus sustain the local boom for years to come. Marathon Oil, for instance, plans on spending $1.5 billion to drill 300 new wells over the next few years.

Like a modern gold rush, all this feverish activity hearkens to the 1870s, when miners came pouring into South Dakota's Black Hills in search of gold.

FOLLOWING PAGES | *The Glucksdahl Lutheran Church in Bentley, North Dakota, is one of hundreds of abandoned churches across the region.*

In short, the U.S. Army's announcement of gold in 1874 brought an invasion of prospectors and settlers into lands that had been set aside for the Indians. Chief Red Cloud's tireless efforts had resulted in an 1868 treaty that created the Great Sioux Reservation, which covered basically all of western South Dakota. Now settlers began moving in, violating the treaty, and serious conflicts arose.

THE GHOST DANCE AND THE POWWOW

IN 1877 THE GOVERNMENT SIMPLY BOWED to the inevitable tide of settlers and reneged on the 1868 treaty. The Indians would have to move to smaller reservations or fight against the Army. For a while, chiefs such as Sitting Bull and Crazy Horse waged war—at times successfully—but eventually most of the Sioux surrendered and moved to the reservations. The buffalo that had sustained their way of life were nearly depleted anyway. The railroad had divided them into southern and northern herds. Professional hunters came through and killed as many buffalo as they could from a single spot to make it easy for skinners to do their job. The skinners would turn the animals on their backs, cut them jaw to tail, stretch the hides out flat, and leave them to cure. In the spring the hides were loaded onto wagons and shipped to eastern markets for tanning. In addition to the market for hides, buffalo were slaughtered in massive numbers as a way of forcing the Indians from roaming the Plains. Sioux holy man Black Elk was baffled by the killing: "They killed them for the metal that makes them crazy, and they took only the hides to sell. Sometimes they did not even take the hides, only the tongues. . . . You can see that the men who did this were crazy." Without their lifeline, the Indians had to adapt to white ways or starve.

A Paiute holy man named Wovoka came along in 1889 and began a religious revival. He prophesied that the white people would leave and the buffalo return if the Indians performed what was called the Ghost Dance. After years of losing battles with the U.S. Army, after seeing their old ways die in a matter of four decades, the Sioux were willing to try anything. They began Ghost Dancing. Night and day they danced in their muslin, "bullet proof" shirts until they dropped with exhaustion and had visions of dead relatives. Whites living near the reservations got nervous; the U.S. Army sent troops to quell what they considering an uprising.

When the Lakota danced, they sang in achingly beautiful poetry:

OPPOSITE | *Purifying the area with bundled sage, William Brave Bull prays at the graves of his ancestors near Wakpala, South Dakota.*

The whole world is coming,
A nation is coming, a nation is coming.
The eagle has brought the message
to the tribe.
The father says so, the father says so.
Over the whole earth they are coming.
The buffalo are coming,
the buffalo are coming,
Give me back my bow.

The buffalo were not ever coming again. One of the principal Sioux leaders, Sitting Bull was arrested at his encampment on South Dakota's Standing Rock Reservation. He briefly struggled and was killed (see sidebar, pp. 96-97). Tension mounted among the Sioux, and another leader, Chief Big Foot, headed from the Cheyenne River, in the south part of the reservation, to

On his 1874 excursion into the Black Hills, General Custer (seated) and a soldier meet with three Arikara scouts, who would fight with Custer's army against the Sioux in the 1876 Battle of Little Bighorn.

In 1908, Crow scouts revisit the Little Bighorn, the scene of Custer's defeat in 1876. The Crow helped the U.S. Army protect their lands from the Sioux, yet in the end all tribes succumbed to waves of white settlement.

Pine Ridge where he hoped to join forces with Chief Red Cloud. A detachment of the U.S. Cavalry met up with the ragged, cold band of 350 Indians and escorted them to an encampment along Wounded Knee Creek. In the morning the Indians were ordered to give up their weapons; during a tent search a shot was fired. In the ensuing melee, 200 Indian men, women, and children were killed. About 25 of the 500 soldiers died.

At first billed as a "battle," the episode soon became known far and wide as a brutal massacre, with whites joining in the condemnation. The long and bitter struggle of whites against Indians throughout North America was over at last. "Who would have thought that dancing could make such trouble?" said Chief Short Bull. "For the message I brought was peace."

In the years after Wounded Knee, Indian dancing came back. Entertainers such as Buffalo Bill Cody particularly sought Indians who had fought against the U.S. Cavalry, and thus, ironically, competitive powwow dancing has its roots as much in Wild West shows as in ancient tradition. Dancing became so popular among the Indians that, in 1923, the commissioner of Indian Affairs issued an

Lake Ilo National Wildlife Refuge

In a region not known for its abundance of water, a good lake stands out like a life preserver to the migratory birds that fly through twice a year. Such a place is Lake Ilo National Wildlife Refuge, more than 4,000 acres of prairie, grasslands, and wetlands surrounding a 1,200-acre lake. Situated near Dunn Center, North Dakota, the refuge came about when a dam was built in 1936 at the confluence of Murphy and Spring Creeks as a Works Progress Administration project. The refuge was established three years later as a breeding ground for birds and other wildlife.

About 226 species of birds use the lake at least part of the year; on some autumn days up to 100,000 waterfowl gather here. Canada geese mass on the little islands, facing the steady, whitecap-stirring winds, while Chinese ring-neck pheasants stroll casually across roads. Though they can fly, pheasants often don't bother and are hit along highways. Other refuge birds include grebes, cormorants, herons, bitterns, killdeer, and a variety of ducks. Among mammals are white-tailed deer, beaver, badger, skunk, and mink. Occasionally you can spot a pronghorn here; the Western Hemisphere's fastest animal, they can bound along at up to 70 miles per hour.

When the water level was lowered seven feet in 1989 during dam repairs, the lake bed revealed some rare archaeological treasures. Several Paleo-Indian sites, dating back 10,500 years, lay scattered about. Perhaps the most interesting find was a tepee ring, or stone circle, that had remained undisturbed under vegetation and topsoil; the stones supported the poles of a tepee perhaps 500 years ago. Among 58,000 artifacts collected were hearth stones, pottery shards, and spear and arrow points. Many tools were made from flint gathered at nearby Knife River, while others were of petrified wood from Rainy Buttes, 80 miles away. Today a reconstruction of the tepee ring sits at the lake's edge.

open letter to "all Indians" asking them not to neglect their stock and crops, torture their bodies, handle poisonous snakes, indulge in drugs or gambling, or give away money or property during ceremonies. "I could issue an order against these useless and harmful performances," he wrote, "but I would much rather have you give them up of your own free will."

These days body torture is limited to private sun dances, while powwows are celebrations open to the public. I learned a great deal about Indian culture by attending the United Tribes International Powwow, the largest powwow of the Northern Plains. Held at the United Tribes Technical College outside Bismarck, the powwow has been an annual event since 1969 and now attracts some 1,000 dancers and drummers from tribes around the country. I was one of 20,000 spectators at the four-day event.

The powwow was held outdoors in a round arena, signifying the circle of life; dancers entered from the west, in Sioux tradition. Craft and food booths formed an outer circle. A few people took pictures, but many more held tape recorders up near the drummers and

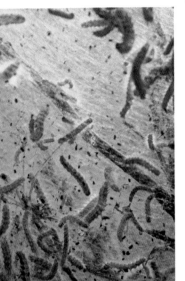

Tent caterpillars weave webs in the Little Missouri National Grasslands.

singers—the music was what they wanted to take home. The atmosphere was festive, celebratory; the competition—up to $1,200 for top prizes—was only part of what was going on. "The powwow is about gathering, about making friends," Ron Eagle Chasing told me. "If you win, you win; if you don't, you don't. It's really about sharing the knowledge with the younger generation. They carry it on, and that way we keep the culture and traditional values alive."

Ron was one of the scariest looking dancers I could find. As a buffalo dancer, he wore a horned headpiece topped with an eagle head and decorated with ermine tails; his breastplate was of buffalo bone, his bustle of eagle feathers, his face painted red and white. I could not help staring at his outfit. "It's a buffalo dream headdress," he said, "with an eagle that carries prayers to heaven twenty-four seven, not just on Sunday. The breastplate wards off bullets. The tails are because I come from a chief.

FOLLOWING PAGES | *Spectators ponder which participants will win the Elgin Days turtle races in Elgin, North Dakota, population 2,300.*

Welcome to our town: Marie Lorge greets visitors to Georges and the Owl Café in the tiny, out-of-the-way hamlet of Amidon, North Dakota. With a population of 17, Amidon ranks as the nation's smallest county seat.

Each feather you earn by deeds or in battle." He told me he participates in the senior men's traditional dance, which tells the story of a battle or a hunt. Other dance categories include grass, fancy, and jingle, each identifiable by the dancer's regalia.

Ron is from Eagle Butte, South Dakota, in the Cheyenne River Reservation. The longer we talked, the more he revealed of his life, which in turn opened a fascinating glimpse into the heart of the Native American experience. At 60 years old, he has been married nine times. "And been in eight car wrecks," he said, the first of which killed his first wife. "I grew up beer-drinking, womanizing, running around—a real cowboy." But it was his duty in Vietnam that most shaped his outlook, and he kept returning to it in our discussion.

A gunner with the 161st aviation company, Ron flew missions with Korean marines. "They had a take-no-prisoners policy, and I was very honored to support them." He claims to have killed 43 people in battle and to have taken scalps. "A Lakota warrior goes to die for his people. It's an honor to die. He doesn't ask why he's fighting." He talked about

Shoes anyone? Roman Fettig awaits customers at his shoe store in Crosby, North Dakota. Soon to close, the store is a veritable museum of unmoved inventory dating as far back as the 1950s.

the people who spat on returning soldiers and about having flashbacks when he heard gunshots or fireworks and how therapy had helped him come to terms with his war years. Yet the most helpful thing in overcoming his post-traumatic stress disorder, as he himself called it, seems to have been his native religion. "I tried Mormon, Catholic, Episcopal, Baptist, but I came back to my own—the sweat lodge, the Sun Dance, Wakan Tanka." He defined Wakan Tanka, the Lakota god, as "the creator" or "the great mystery." The term "savior" did not come up, and I wondered if living out on a reservation made the natural world seem foremost among God's manifestations or if that were simply a Lakota way of looking at the divinity.

"I made my commitment to the creator," Ron said, explaining the most sacred ritual, the sun dance. He begins preparing for the summer ritual in the fall, cutting out meals, then going whole days without eating. At the core of the 12-day ceremony is a 4-day period of fasting, during which the participant remains within a small circle. During traditional rituals, participants were pierced in the breast with a sliver of bone attached to a leather thong and

hoisted until they broke free; the self-inflicted pain was an offering to Wakan Tanka and a symbol of death and rebirth. Banned in the early 1900s, the practice has crept back into the Sun Dance of some tribes. "It's not painful, because you're in a constant state of spirituality," Ron said. "You say prayers for humility and pity." He points to his chest where he bears scars from previous dances, as proud of them as if they were battle wounds.

He moved randomly from one topic to the next, speaking in short, declarative bursts, using the fingers of his hand to explain such things as the five stages of life, and pointing to some nearby cottonwoods as a metaphor for how we grow. He would make little jokes and explain that humor is part of the Lakota way. He told me he was from the Mniconju band of the Lakota, making sure I spelled it right, and said that his Indian name is Kills the Enemy. He said he was descended from Crazy Horse and a man named Chief Hump. He has 27 children and numerous grandchildren.

Another dancer I spoke with said he danced for the exercise, but Ron seemed to have a deeper purpose. It was a social gathering, but it was also a religious ceremony. And it was a chance to wear a costume that connected him to his long past here on the Dakota plains and proclaimed, *I am a Lakota elder and an American warrior at peace with who I am.* Beneath the regalia was a balding, overweight veteran with a troubled past, but as a buffalo dancer he was a dignified warrior again, happy to share his knowledge with a nosy outsider like myself. For a while he transported us both back 150 years, the drums and the wailing songs vibrating the air around us.

Then it was time for him to dance, to go keep the old ways alive. He went into the arbor, the arena's inner circle, with the other senior men who had made the cut. The drumming started up again, and Ron Eagle Chasing danced, "to look like I'm sneaking up on somebody," he'd said, "and making it to the next battle." By the end he was out of breath. I didn't stay to see if he'd won—that had never really been the point anyway.

Saddles are welcome trophies at the Elgin Rodeo, in Elgin, North Dakota.

OPPOSITE | *Jake and Sam McAlpin practice roping and posing skills in Grassy Butte, North Dakota, a community sustained by ranchers.*

A calf gets branded on Gary Jepson's ranch in Killdeer, North Dakota. Some 250 calves were rounded up, separated from their mothers, branded, and inoculated on this cold May day.

OLD–TIME SADDLE MAKER

DRIVING ACROSS THE NORTH DAKOTA plains one cold morning, I saw nothing for miles but big round bales of hay scattered about the neatly sculpted hills like pieces of shredded-wheat cereal, so many that after a while their placement began to seem purposeful, as if they were pieces on a giant's game board. The sky is so huge that even individual clouds can seem imbued with significance and meaning. Steam rose from the bales, wind shimmering the grasses and buffeting the car. I stopped briefly in Amidon, seat of Slope County. The one restaurant was closed; there was also an antiques shop, a Lutheran church, some abandoned houses, and not much else. At the undistinguished building that serves as a courthouse, I asked for tourist information. The clerks were friendly, though somewhat at a loss. "Well, we have White Butte out our back door." The highest point in North Dakota, the 3,506-foot prominence rises quite visibly about 5 miles to the south. A local farmer sang out helpfully, "Amidon, Amidon, a pimple on the asshole of the world." The town's population peaked at 162 in 1930, declining to 26 by the 2000 census, making it the smallest county seat in the nation. Not quite a complete ghost town,

Master of a dying art, custom saddle maker Bill Engen stands in his shop outside Belfield, North Dakota. Bill's hand-tooled saddles, made only to order, sell for around $2,000 and are designed to last a lifetime.

it continues on into an uncertain future, the oil boom having for now passed Slope County by.

There were plenty of other Amidons around, but I wanted to see something alive. Throughout the western Dakotas, the art and craft of ranching is alive and well, not simply a subject for television drama. The great open-range roundups in the Dakotas started in 1881 and were over by 1902. In general the Dakota territory did not suffer the kinds of savage range wars between cattlemen and sheepherders that took place in other regions, but cowboys still had the same jobs—rounding up, roping, branding, patrolling the range or fence line (in good weather and bad), and sometimes breaking horses. And there were always corrals to build, fences to mend, waterholes to check, and sick and injured animals to look after—pretty much the same jobs it takes to maintain a herd of cattle today. The more versatile and knowledgeable a cowhand is, the more useful.

These days, in addition to horses, ranchers rely on jeeps, trucks, and even airplanes and helicopters to manage their property. While the Dakotas hold more than 60,000

FOLLOWING PAGES | *Eyes on the prize, a horse and rider charge to within roping range of steer at the two-day Elgin Rodeo in North Dakota.*

Dr. Thomas E. Jacobsen of Hettinger, North Dakota, visits the home of patients he delivered. Though not technically a house call, such drop-in check-ups are common practice among the small-town doctors in his clinic.

farms and ranches, the farms tend to lie in the east and the ranches in the west, the latter ranging from a few thousand acres to about 75,000 acres. In the western Dakotas, cattle are generally raised for beef, sheep for wool; in addition, winter wheat is grown on a large scale in southwestern South Dakota. On a typical cattle ranch, such as Gary Jepson's in Killdeer, North Dakota, some 250 calves will be branded on a spring day. The brandings are social as well as working events, which can draw dozens of friends and neighbors to help with the work, share food, and catch up on the news.

Probably the most exciting action associated with ranching are events that showcase the cowboy's and cowgirl's skills—rodeos. About 50 professional and amateur rodeos take place every year across the Dakotas, some of them part of larger fairs and festivals that offer rodeo events as a main draw. Back in the early days, cowboys who still had energy after a long day's cattle drive or roundup would entertain each other by competing to see who was the best at steer roping and bronc riding and so forth. Eventually the sport became formalized, and spectators were charged a fee to see the show in an arena. Today riders still compete in steer roping and bronc riding, as well as bareback bronc riding, bull riding, calf roping, team steer roping, and steer wrestling.

Women compete in barrel racing and sometimes other events. In barrel racing, contestants ride a cloverleaf pattern around three barrels as fast as possible. Among the most thrilling events are women's bronc and bull (or steer) riding. Instead of the eight seconds required for men, women must stay on the twisting, leaping bull for six seconds and can hold with both hands the rope that encircles the bull. But those are often six of the longest seconds you'll ever see, and the women who stay on are among the toughest.

After taking in the rodeo at Elgin, I headed northwest to visit the workshop of saddler Bill Engen. Right off he began telling me about a mishap at the Fourth of July parade in Medora, as a way of explaining a limp I probably wouldn't have noticed. His horse got impatient and bucked. "He didn't throw me, but he rearranged me some, reintroduced

Like a big family, students at the one-room Sweetbriar School near Mandan, North Dakota, take time out for recreation. In operation since 1942, the school current tops out with an enrollment of 11 students.

Despite a population of under 1,000 (and falling), Crosby, North Dakota, keeps its 1938 movie theater in operation. The ornate Divide County Courthouse presides at the end of the street.

me to the saddle horn. After that he was the best horse in the parade. I snapped my back, pulled my groin, was black and blue in places I don't talk about. Don't heal as fast as I used to. He didn't dump me though. I was pretty much shuffling like Tim Conway, then long about August I was back in the shop."

Bill's a short fellow with cowboy boots and hat, jeans, long mustache, a colorful way of speaking, but a modest manner. He's the authentic article—his beautifully handmade work does the boasting for him. He showed me the saddles he made for his family, each with intricate tooling. His wife's rose-motif saddle and bridle are outfitted with $400 worth of jewels;

his granddaughter's saddle is worked with a horse-head image. Another saddle has a leaf pattern; one with eagles sells for about $2,000. In one corner of the shop, he is restoring an old army saddle, while at the same time he is making a saddle from scratch. Starting with a ponderosa-pine saddletree, he adds four layers of leather to get exactly the right feel. All the work is made to order and hand-stitched. He estimates there are no more than 40 saddle makers in the United States who "do it the old-time way."

He especially likes the tooling work. "I like to make 'em fancy," he says, then he shows me a saddle with a simple barbed-wire motif. "This is as fancy as

Couples mingle for contra, swing, and square dancing at a barn dance near Hazen, North Dakota. Held about six times a year, these old-fashioned mixers give young people a chance to meet and socialize.

they get anymore." At a cowboy poetry gathering recently he displayed some of his work. "And all those tough ranchers said, 'Oh, no, that's too pretty— I wouldn't ride that.' I wanted to show 'em I could make a plain, ugly one, too. But just cause it's pretty don't mean it ain't tough. You're buying an heirloom as far as I'm concerned—your great-grandson's gonna ride it."

Bill grew up in the Pacific Northwest and apprenticed right out of high school in Oregon. "And then the old saddle maker up and died. So then I thought I was gonna be a rodeo star for a couple of years. I rode rough stock all over, wherever I hung my hat." During a

stint in the Navy he made extra money riding at an Old West theme park in Virginia Beach. "I rode the same horse and same bull once a night and twice on Sunday, so they'd know what I was gonna do and I'd know what they were gonna do. After eight seconds we was just friendly as hell together. I realized I ain't gonna make any money there, ain't no future in it for me. That was back before you had sponsors—you were just on your own."

It was also in the navy that he got his nickname, with which he often inscribes his saddles. He was on a swift boat in Vietnam. Of the six men, two were named Bill. The other Bill, whom they called "Bighorse," was six foot three. "One day the skipper asked for Bill, and somebody said, 'Bighorse Bill?' The skipper said, 'No, Ponybill.' So ever since then I got stuck with Ponybill, and it fits because of my size. Didn't bother me."

After his rodeo years he found another saddle maker to apprentice to, and 45 years later he is still making saddles. He briefly retired a few years ago, but got tired of fishing and drinking beer and returned to what he loves best. He also likes helping young people—taking on students or doing repairs for area rodeo riders who don't have a lot of money. Over the years he's had three

A rusting old flatbed and a derelict house under a lowering sky make for a typically stark and nostalgic scene in Divide County, North Dakota, which faces a dwindling population and uncertain future.

apprentices, two of whom went on to become saddle makers, and upwards of 20 part-time students.

We talk on for a while, Bill showing me an old-style roping saddle and a pair of bull-nosed tapideros he made to cover a rider's feet and stirrups. The smell and creak of the leather, Bill's voice, his tools, an old sheepherder's cookstove he stokes for heat—all of it evokes an Old West that has not died. A sign on the wall reads: "The best thing for the inside of a man is the outside of a horse." But Bill tells me his favorite Will Rogers line is "Don't squat with your spurs on."

Asked if he makes English saddles, the answer is a quick "no." Is there no call for them? "I wouldn't make 'em if there was a call for 'em. I'm just an old cowboy."

I ask if his children or grandchildren are interested in learning the trade. He shakes his head. "I'd like 'em to learn," he says. "But one thing I've learned over the years is you don't get rich being a saddle maker. Anyway they live in the modern world. I live a hundred years back."

BEAR BUTTE TREK

I HEADED SOUTH, TO A PLACE THAT GOES way back in history, and prehistory. Rising abruptly more than 1,000 feet above the South Dakota plains near the Black Hills, Bear Butte has long been a kind of Mecca for many Indian nations. Instead of a true flat-topped butte, the double-humped, sleeping-bear-shaped peak is an upthrust of volcanic rock. The Lakota, Cheyenne, Mandan, Arikara, Kiowa, Crow, Arapaho, and others have creation stories and other myths that spring from Bear Butte. To this day many Native Americans consider it as sacred as the Vatican: On any given week there might be a half dozen worshipers seeking visions or engaging in other religious rites on the mountain. That the peak is contained within a state park presents both an opportunity and a challenge for Indians who want to preserve its sanctity.

"It's a shrine," says park manager Jim Jandreau, a Lakota Indian. "There's no dogs allowed, no beer, no hunting. What church would you do that in? If somebody has a gun in church, it has its own power. Your focus won't be on your prayers." As we talk, someone lets a dog loose in the parking lot, and Jim has to pause to handle the matter. In the car, the dog whines miserably, and Jim's point becomes crystal clear. He continues, adamant about Bear Butte and the need to educate people about its importance. He shows me a plaque honoring an Army captain who camped in the vicinity in 1859. "He wasn't even here, he was *near* here. A lot of things are wrong, and they need to be corrected. A dominant culture has imprinted on what was here."

SITTING BULL

❧

I never taught my people to trust the Americans. I have told them the truth—that the Americans are great liars. I have never dealt with the Americans. Why should I? The land belonged to my people."

Hunkpapa Sioux Chief Sitting Bull (Tatanka Iyotake) was born around 1831 in the Dakota Territory near Grand River. Settlers had been slowly moving into the territory, and during his lifetime he was to witness the demise of the Sioux Nation while serving as one of its greatest spiritual leaders.

In 1863 he participated in a skirmish with federal troops; a year later he was fighting again at the Battle of Kildeer Mountain, in which Gen. Alfred Sully's 2,200 troops dispersed a Sioux encampment of some 6,000 warriors in retaliation for an uprising in Minnesota. By the time gold was discovered in the Black Hills in 1874, Sitting Bull had become an outspoken and articulate critic of the white settlers who were now flocking to the region in violation of an 1868 treaty. "We want no white men here," he said. "The Black Hills belong to me. If the whites try to take them, I will fight."

When the Sioux were ordered onto reservations in 1875, Sitting Bull refused. In a vision during a Sun Dance he saw soldiers falling like grasshoppers from the sky. The following year, while trying to track down Sitting Bull's warriors, Gen. George Custer and 211 cavalrymen were annihilated by a larger Sioux encampment on the Little Bighorn River in southeastern Montana. Though some national sympathy was aroused for the Indians, the general tide was against them. The Army's new tactic was to gradually wear the Indians down and starve them out. The near extinction of the buffalo drove many to surrender.

"We kill buffaloes as we kill other animals, for food and clothing, and to make our lodges warm," Sitting Bull said. "They kill buffaloes—for what? Go through the country. See the thousands of carcasses rotting on the Plains. Your young men shoot for pleasure. . . . You call us savages. What are *they*?" In May 1877 he and his dwindling band decamped for Canada.

Four years later Sitting Bull and his followers, tired and famished, returned to the Dakota Territory and surrendered at Fort Buford. In 1883 he moved to the Standing Rock Reservation, where he continued to speak against the selling of Sioux land. For a while he traveled with Buffalo Bill Cody's Wild West Show, signing autographs for 50 cents apiece. When the Ghost Dance movement—predicting the demise of the whites

SITTING BULL'S FAMILY.

COPYRIGHTED BY D. F. BARRY 1891.

Sitting Bull's family gathers outside their tepee in 1891, shortly after the death of the great Sioux chief.
OPPOSITE | *Arrows found at the Little Bighorn battlefield were shot by Indians hiding in gullies, unseen by soldiers.*

and the return of the buffalo—came to the Dakotas in 1890, Indian police were sent to arrest Sitting Bull as a precaution. He was living again near the Grand River on the Standing Rock Reservation. The police arrived on the morning of December 15; Sitting Bull was asleep on the floor of his lodge with his two wives. When his son accused him of complying with the police, the chief resisted and in the struggle he was shot in the back and killed. A gunfight ensued that left seven of Sitting Bull's followers and four policemen dead. In a jarringly comic note, Sitting Bull's show horse, cued by the gunfire, began doing tricks.

The death of Sitting Bull was followed two weeks later by the massacre at Wounded Knee. The Sioux resistance was over.

Jim tells me that most people who live nearby are bigoted, to use his term, but that there are also "some really good people and they're coming on board, seeing this place as sacred, questioning why a motorcycle rally has to be held at the foot of the mountain." (The rally he refers to is an annual weeklong event held in nearby Sturgis.) "The Indian religion is not a religion, it's a way of life. We burn sage and are called heathen. When the Catholics burn incense it's okay—there's still a double standard. Even to talk about spirituality is something we don't do as Americans. It's almost something we're ashamed of, as though we're better than that."

Indians often come to Bear Butte on vision quests in preparation for the following year's Sun Dance. They will stay in one place on the mountain, with nothing but a buffalo robe for shelter, praying and fasting for four days, until achieving a trance-like release from the body. Jim personally does not fast here because of what he calls a "circus atmosphere." "The harmony that should be here isn't—the spirits are not as settled as they used to be." Although there are not many visitors here at mid-morning, the longer we talk, the more people arrive; just after noon a bus pulls up and disgorges a load of passengers. The place became a park in 1961, and the irony, Jim tells me, is that it did not become popular until more Indians started coming.

I decide to take a walk to the top. Jim claimed he used to be able to make the three and a half miles in fifty minutes—he had to jog down. It's a rigorous, switchbacking trail, and I don't plan on walking so fast. There are no vision questers on the mountain today, but all along the trail are colorful prayer cloths tied to scrubby pines. Some are bandanas, others simply strips of shirt; some contain little pouches of tobacco—all of them representing prayers for healing, guidance, the happiness of friends and family. The trail gains elevation so quickly I begin seeing spots. Heart drumming furiously, I make it to the top. There's a magnificent panorama all around of plaid fields, little lakes, and the Black Hills off to the southwest. I try to picture what it was like long ago—no roads, more untamed grass, but still the same exhilarating, limitless view.

"Even the Crows used to come here at one time," Jim told me. "They were dread enemies of the Lakota, but here they were treated like family." It was a kind of neutral island in the vast sea of the Plains, and though many Indians would not go to the top, the creator's roof, they could come to Bear Butte and know they were home.

OPPOSITE | *Like a divining rod for morning light, deer antlers take on a roseate hue in North Dakota's Little Missouri National Grassland.*

CHAPTER THREE

BADLANDS

THE WILDEST DAKOTAS

The Badlands look as you might expect the moon to look if it were hot, a parched picture of the Earth in exploding wrath. It is as if it were the devil's own bit of the planet and he had stabbed and slashed with some great knife until all fertility drained away from yawning wounds." The description is from British travel writer Douglas Reed in 1951. John Steinbeck likened the badlands to "the work of an evil child." The Indians called them *mako sica*, the French *les mauvaises terres*, both of which mean bad lands for traveling. Others have been drawn to their surreal beauty. Forbidding, lonely, otherworldly—the badlands inspire strong reaction one way or another from nearly everybody who comes across them.

Theodore Roosevelt used this Maltese Cross branding iron on his ranch near Medora, North Dakota.
OPPOSITE | *Cottonwoods show autumn finery in Theodore Roosevelt National Park.*
PREVIOUS PAGES | *Eroded buttes of Badlands National Park make for many a scenic backdrop.*

PRIMARILY LOCATED SOUTHEAST OF South Dakota's Black Hills and along North Dakota's Little Missouri River, the badlands are interruptions in the smooth flow of the plains. As though a giant had left a few waffle-soled footprints, the land suddenly drops away into a fantastical, eroded netherworld of wrinkled domes, striped peaks, and dry, twisting gullies. Weather tends toward the extremes: The mercury can top 110°F and dip below –35°F; a fast-moving storm might drop the temperature 40 degrees in a few hours. And always there is the wind—warm in summer, cold in winter.

Near Interior, South Dakota, layered buttes in Badlands National Park are incised by gullies and washes, while oxidized iron creates reddish tints. These soft clays and silts weather quickly in geological terms.

Prickly pear cactus is found throughout the badlands; its red fruit provides food for wildlife, and its yellow flowers accent a sere landscape. Cactus are among the few plants that live on sun-baked southern slopes.

Perspectives on the badlands appear to have changed over time. In 1842, they were an obstacle to explorers like John C. Fremont: "I had never seen anything which impressed so strongly on my mind a feeling of desolation. . . . The wind was high and bleak; the barren, arid country seemed as if it had been swept by fires, and in every direction the same dull ash-colored hue derived from the formation met the eye. . . . We left the place with pleasure." Yet just over a century later, Pulitzer-winning writer Wallace Stegner waxed poetic: "There was never a country that in its good moments was more beautiful. Even in drought or dust storm or blizzard, it is the reverse of monotonous, once you have submitted to it with all the senses. You don't get out of the wind, but learn to lean and squint against it. You don't escape sky and sun, but wear them in your eyeballs and on your back. You become acutely aware of yourself. The world is very large, the sky even larger, and you are very small."

FOLLOWING PAGES | *Rugged buttes and shadows form a badlands battlement hundreds of feet high, suggesting a Martian landscape.*

With fewer wild places than in Fremont's time, the "badlands" now connote a Bruce Springsteen song of the same name, or the kind of "badness" that lures white-collar motorcyclists on holiday, nature lovers, and all aficionados of rugged, extraterrestrial terrain.

BADLANDS NATIONAL PARK

SOUTH DAKOTA'S BADLANDS NATIONAL Park makes it somewhat easy to dive into the scenery, whether you see it from behind your windshield or actually get out onto a trail. I took some short trails on a 95-degree day recently, and found myself plunged almost right away into the mako sica. One trail was so steep, the footing so loose and crumbly, I almost fell several times. It was far too rough for the homesteaders' rigs. In order to pay a visit to the little town of Interior, they had to park their wagons on the ridgeline at the top and coax their horses down. Some of those hardy souls may have paused to take in the gorgeous vista—tablelands spread far to the north, while to the south a vast, gulping space opens out to the White River Valley and beyond.

OPPOSITE | *Emily and Sammi Comes cradle kittens on their grandfather Gary Tennant's ranch in Camp Crook, South Dakota.*
FOLLOWING PAGES | *Gary Tennant monitors his sheep—5,000 all told—by airplane.*

Fence-mending is one of many endless chores on a sheep ranch just outside the badlands; this 19,000-acre ranch, run by Gary Tennant (above) and his son, has some 80 miles of fencing.

Other trails give views of buttes 25 miles away, while close at hand all around are pyramids and cones of sand and clay banded in pinks, browns, yellows, and chalky white. While not much grows on the sun-blasted south-facing slopes, on the more protected northern sides junipers and sage and prairie grasses make little scented gardens, where rabbits and big-eared mule deer browse contentedly. One trail runs to the top of a spectacular canyon, upon which shadows are projected by late afternoon sun. Another ends in a view of an ancient metropolis of spires and hoodoos in the most preposterous, Suessian shapes—a huge mushroom, a row of gnarled tepees, a miniature capitol with subterranean passages, the prow of a ship breasting the wind. It made me want to go striding across it on giant legs.

Skulls decorate the Longhorn Saloon in the ghost town of Scenic, South Dakota.

Relatively young in geological terms, the Badlands began eroding about 500,000 years ago (Grand Canyon erosion dates back 5 million years). On the other hand, the layers—visible everywhere in multicolored bands—were deposited as far back as 75 million years ago. The oldest layer, the Pierre Shale, was laid down in the Cretaceous Period when a shallow, inland sea covered much of the present Great Plains. With the gradual uplift of the Rockies, the sea drained off and the exposed mud weathered into a yellow soil known as the Yellow Mounds Layer. Then, about 35 million years ago, the area held a great river floodplain and subtropical forest; each flooding deposited another layer of the gray Chadron Formation. Mammal fossils found in this layer include the rhinoceros-like titanotheres. A few million years later, during the Oligocene Epoch, the climate became cooler and drier, and an open savannah began replacing the forest. The associated layer is the light-brown Brule Formation, which holds numerous mammal fossils. Some 26 to 28 million years old, the whitish Sharps Formation is visible at the jagged tops of peaks; it consists of 30 feet of ash—blown here from volcanoes to the west—and 150 feet of river sediments.

About five million years ago, with the final uplift of the Rocky Mountains and the Black Hills, the Great Plains were elevated and streams began slicing downward through the layers.

Badlands National Park's South Unit

Most visitors to Badlands National Park drive some of the north unit's loop road and stop for a couple of overlooks or short walks. Yet the majority of the park lies in the undeveloped south unit within the Pine Ridge Indian Reservation; the park service and the Oglala Lakota manage the area together. These 130,000 acres feature the same kinds of rugged buttes and broken lands, while retaining a more untamed, Wild West feel.

From the hole-in-the-wall town of Scenic, a county road dips briefly into the south unit. A rough dirt road—which turns to wheel-spinning mush in the rain—runs for about seven jouncing miles across rutted flats and up a dizzying cliff to Sheep Mountain Table. Those who make it to the juniper grove at the end of the road are treated to one of the park's greatest views—from a high point of windswept land you can behold a jaw-dropping array of pinnacles and spires and crenellated fins.

To the south, another even more rutted track leads out to Stronghold Table via miles of lonely grasslands. There is a good possibility of getting lost along the way to what is an unremarkable view. The goal, though, is to reach the place where the Sioux held their last Ghost Dance in December 1890, shortly before the massacre at nearby Wounded Knee Creek. Believers danced until they fell into trances and dropped with exhaustion into the snow, filled with visions of a messiah coming to clear out the whites and bring back the buffalo. The Lakota still consider this a sacred place. Not quite as sacred, the adjoining Galigo Table was acquired from the Lakota during World War II for use as a bombing and gunnery range. Returned to the Indians after 20 years, the land still contains unexploded ordinance.

To get to the even less accessible Palmer Creek Unit, you have to spend at least two days hiking in and out, and since you're crossing private land to get there, you need an alternate route in case landowners deny you access.

The Little Missouri River snakes through the north unit of Theodore Roosevelt National Park, where wind and water continue the work of some 600,000 years, carving the soft sedimentary deposits.

The glacial ice sheets of one to two million years ago never extended to the badlands, but they pushed the Missouri River down into the Dakotas. Then about half a million years ago, the Cheyenne River (a Missouri tributary) began draining streams from the Black Hills that had once replenished the badlands with sediment. After that, all these soft, sedimentary layers of sand, silt, and clay began eroding fairly quickly in the wind and rain—about an inch per year. At this rate the badlands will likely be gone within another 500,000 years.

A tremendous number of fossils have been found in the area. The Oligocene was a time when strange animals roamed the grasslands that became the badlands. This was home to the mesohippus, a coyote-size three-toed horse; the merycoidon, a kind of fanged sheep; the hyaenodon, which looked somewhat like an African hyena; a big land tortoise called the stylemys; and the archaeotherium—a super-size

At the Castles near present-day Reva, South Dakota, the 1876 Battle of Slim Buttes occurred shortly after the Battle of Little Bighorn. Crazy Horse and 2,000 Sioux warriors fought a U.S. Army unit to a draw.

boar with a four-foot-long head and tusks. And there were ancient mammals resembling modern saber-tooth cats, rabbits, and squirrels.

The badlands extend beyond park boundaries into private lands, Buffalo Gap National Grassland, and the Pine Ridge Indian Reservation. The largest reservation in the Dakotas at 1.8 million acres, Pine Ridge is second in size only to Arizona's Navajo Reservation. Scattered among the reservation's prairies and broken lands are tiny towns focused around a gas station, trading post, and laundromat. Elsewhere among vast stretches of emptiness are clutches of double-wides and sheds, strung together by telephone wires, then nothing again for miles except cattle, buttes, and dry washes.

In the south part of the reservation, a cemetery on a hill above the Red Cloud Indian Mission School holds the grave

FOLLOWING PAGES | *A summer thunderstorm draws a curtain on the sky in North Dakota's Little Missouri National Grassland.*

No. 3691. "Red Cloud and American Horse." The two most noted Chiefs now living. Photo and copyright '91 by Grabill, P. & V. Co., Deadwood, S. D.

THE GRABILL PORTRAIT AND VIEW CO., DEADWOOD, S. D.

Our Company is incorporated under State Laws.   Views all Copyrighted.   Will give a handsome reward for detection of anyone copying our pictures.

of Chief Red Cloud. Born in 1822, Red Cloud became one of the most powerful and effective leaders of the Oglala Teton Sioux. For a while, he was able to slow the pace of white incursion.

In 1865, to protect his people's traditional hunting grounds, he led contingents of Sioux and Cheyenne against U.S. Army troops who were building a road from Ft. Laramie in Wyoming to the goldfields of Montana. His warriors intercepted the construction workers and held them for two weeks. Afterward, he refused to negotiate with government commissioners. Military posts were then built to protect the workers, and Red Cloud's men went on the warpath. On December 21, 1866, they ambushed and massacred 82 whites. For two years whites and Indians clashed repeatedly in what became known as Red Cloud's War. At a council he told his people, "You have heard the sound of the white soldier's axe upon the Little Piney. His presence here is . . . an insult to the spirits of our ancestors. Are we then to give up their sacred graves to be plowed for corn? Dakotas, I am for war." Finally the government

Wild roses bloom in Theodore Roosevelt National Park's north unit.

agreed to withdraw. Red Cloud saw to the burning of the white men's forts, then signed the Second Treaty of Ft. Laramie in 1868 and moved to the Red Cloud Agency in Nebraska.

Although his followers pursued the war, Red Cloud kept his promise not to fight, moving to the Pine Ridge Agency in 1878. By that point gold had been discovered in the Black Hills and the treaty broken. On trips to Washington, D.C., Red Cloud continued to voice his opposition to government policies. "Whose voice was first sounded on this land?" he asked. "The voice of the red people who had but bows and arrows. . . . What has been done in my country I did not want, did not ask for it; white people going through my country. . . . When the white man comes in my country, he leaves a trail of blood behind him. . . . I have two mountains in that country—the Black Hills and the Big Horn Mountain. I want the Great Father to make no roads through them." Yet in

OPPOSITE | *Oglala Sioux chiefs Red Cloud (in headdress) and American Horse (in Western clothes) shake hands, probably at Pine Ridge.*

acceptance of white culture he and his wife were baptized a few years before his death in 1909.

Red Cloud's grave has a stone botonée cross with a marble relief image of the chief. Attached to the cross, colorful prayer banners flap in the wind. On a horizontal grave slab, pilgrims have placed an assortment of unusual tokens: round stones, cigarette butts held down by stones, bracelets, artificial flowers, a U.S. Marine Corps cap, and a jewelry box containing hair. His wife's grave sits alongside, more modestly marked with a wooden cross.

When I visited, a German and an English couple were there as well, quietly snapping pictures. The English couple had a guide named Joe Whiting. Of Lakota, English, Irish, German, Mexican, and French ancestry, Joe was a shaggy bear of a man who looked like a character from a Louis L'Amour novel—perhaps a buffalo skinner. He wore a wide-brimmed leather hat with a beaded band, high boots, and a long beard. In an indefinably mixed accent he told me that many Europeans are interested in the area because of a 19th-century Austrian novelist named Karl May. "He wrote stories of the Indian as a superhero, like in the Longfellow poems. They read these romantic descriptions of the Old West, the Indians, and the landscape, and they want to come see it for themselves."

WALL AND MINUTEMAN

UP ON THE NORTH SIDE OF BADLANDS National Park, the little town of Wall takes its name from the battlement-like wall of badlands that separates the upper prairie from the White River floodplain. These days the town is better known as the home of Wall Drug. In 1936 the owners of what was once a small drugstore started putting up signs offering free ice water to lure customers. The come-on worked so well that the store expanded over the years into an emporium of little shops, and Wall Drug has become a major tourist stop. Animated quartets sing "Tumblin' Tumbleweed" and other western favorites, while a T. rex and six-foot-high "jackalope" are popular photo-ops. In addition to the kitsch and the various shops—book, jewelry, rock, clothing, and so on—the complex displays hundreds of interesting historical photographs, in no particular order.

A few miles to the southeast, in the grasslands bordering the national park, a chain-link fence encloses a small concrete slab and a few poles. This innocuous-looking place was until the early 1990s the underground den of a weapon that, within about 30 minutes, could have destroyed Moscow, or any other city. There were 150 such sites in

OPPOSITE | *The untrammeled Little Missouri River runs freely through Theodore Roosevelt National Park, and joins the Missouri north of Killdeer.*

South Dakota; today, thanks to the Strategic Arms Reduction Treaty, there are none. This one was preserved—the missile filled with concrete—and the national park service now presents it as a Cold War history lesson.

As I peered into the below-ground silo, Ranger Chris Wilkinson painted a vivid picture of what would have happened in the event this "silent sentinel of the Great Plains" was needed. A four-man crew working in an underground bunker several miles away would punch in the launch codes, the silo would fill with a pressurized gas that would send the concrete lid (the slab I was standing on) flying into the air, and the 57-foot-long missile itself would come shooting out, quickly attaining a speed of 15,000 miles per hour. The outcome you can imagine for yourself. At any given time, each such missile was programmed for six possible targets, mostly intercontinental ballistic missiles in other

Wild horses roam the badlands of Little Missouri Bay Primitive State Park, where the Little Missouri empties into the Missouri River. Visitors can ride, hike, and camp amid striated knobs and pinnacles.

countries. The Minute-man II carried a 1.2 megaton nuclear warhead—equivalent, said Chris, to 60 percent of all the bombs used in World War II.

Looking around, I saw nothing but windblown prairie and distant buttes. And here surrounded by a simple barbed wire fence was Armageddon itself. It was so incongruous I could not really take it in. For one thing the security seemed ludicrous—something out of 1960s middle America, which it was. I could have scaled the fence with a ladder (what I would have done then, I don't know). Chris told me that the alarms were set off numerous times. Crews would come out in the middle of the night and find cows rubbing up against the fences. At the nearby underground launch control facility, the blast door was painted in gallow's humor design: A Domino's pizza box and the words, "Worldwide delivery in 30 minutes or less or your next one's free." I was told each such facility had its own artwork. Some 500 missile sites still dot the Northern Plains, including about 150 near Minot, North Dakota. This crop of ICBMs, though less powerful, is more accurate than the decommissioned ones. Chris described them as "peacekeepers" and "hopefully a deterrent." Hopefully indeed.

From the Cretaceous period, only marine fossils have been found at Badlands National Park—in other words,

no land animals from that far back. For evidence of dinosaurs, you have to travel northwest to a badlands area that straddles South Dakota, North Dakota, and Montana. Here lies exposed the Hell Creek Formation, dating from the end of the age of dinosaurs, about 65 to 67 million years ago. Along here in 1927 the nearly perfect head of a triceratops was excavated by South Dakota's School of Mines. Bones from the giant, long-necked apatosaurus (brontosaurus) and other species have also been found, and many more fossils continue to come to light. Recently a rare mummified hadrosaur was discovered on a ranch near Marmarth, South Dakota. The hadrosaur was a medium-sized, plant-eating bipedal dinosaur with a crested skull and long, flat snout.

THEODORE ROOSEVELT IN THE BADLANDS

In search of more badlands, I traveled on into North Dakota. The badlands here are especially concentrated along the Little Missouri River. I took a drive through the north unit of Theodore Roosevelt National Park to have a look. Along—and in the middle of—the relatively quiet park road was a herd of buffalo, completely unconcerned about a car that weighed only twice what

FOLLOWING PAGES | *The Little Missouri, muddy after a rainfall, meanders through the south unit of Theodore Roosevelt National Park.*

each of them did. Wild horses grazed on a hillside, and all around were more badlands formations similar to those in South Dakota. Erosion in this area, though, has left more rounded shapes, some of them like giant inverted bee-hives, others like melting layer cakes or claws on a clawfoot tub.

I took a five-mile walk up into an area rich in coulees, caprock, and other wonders. The coulees (named by early French fur traders) are dry gulches; during thunderstorms they channel water and sediment down to the Little Missouri. You can see caprock everywhere, studded like jewels into cliffsides, or sitting atop spires like so many pedestals. They are simply harder, more erosion-resistant rock. There are also slumps—tilted mounds that were once part of higher cliffs; like overloaded sand castles, these mounds slide down during wet periods, but you

At river level, canoeists take in the sights of the Little Missouri and its many eroded bluffs and peaks. Bison, wild horses, pronghorn, prairie dogs, bighorn sheep, and other wildlife all depend upon the life-sustaining river.

A cottontail rabbit—capable of leaping 15 feet when animated—hides in tall grasses in Theodore Roosevelt National Park, which offers refuge to a wide variety of wildlife within its 70,000 acres.

can still match their distinctively colored layers with the cliff face higher up. Elsewhere giant cannonball concretions are embedded into cliffs as though they'd been shot there; they are really more like beachball-size pearls or gallstones that form around a hard mineral core.

Sage and yellow rabbitbrush lined the trail, which at high noon was blindingly bright with the badlands' high concentration of sand, silt, and clay. Luckily there were cooler north-facing areas that supported stands of juniper and green ash. Little nine-striped ground squirrels skittered for cover, their tails high; flying grasshoppers snapped their wings. Not much else was moving. Cattle were once

driven right through this impossibly jumbled maze of steep coulees and high terraces. A Texas trail drive in 1884 pushed 4,000 head of longhorn into an open range near here that was vacated by dwindling bison. Thousands of longhorn followed in subsequent drives, but in 20 years they too had gone, victims of overgrazing and hard winters. By 1900, the bison had disappeared from the badlands. Reintroduced into the park in 1956, they have thrived and now number about 400. The park also maintains a small herd of longhorns and reintroduced elk, as well as California bighorn sheep, to replace the extinct Audubon bighorn sheep that once lived here.

Theodore Roosevelt paid for the construction of this three-room log cabin in 1884. Exhibited in Portland and St. Louis during his presidency, the cabin was moved back to the Medora area in 1959.

At the top of the ridge I could see how the badlands had been gouged out of the surrounding plain—the formations all plateau at a uniform height. The huge stillness above all that striped and chiseled busyness below was amazing, considering the amount of work it took to create such a landscape.

Theodore Roosevelt first visited the badlands in September 1883 to hunt buffalo and other big game. He was 24 years old and had recently entered New York state politics. Despite cold and rainy weather, Roosevelt thought the hunt a big success; he loved being outdoors, living a vigorous, rugged life. As a child he had suffered from asthma and frailness, but had worked hard to strengthen himself. By the time he was ready to leave the badlands, he was so intrigued with the area he bought a partnership in the Maltese Cross Ranch, a few miles south of Medora. He supplied the ranch with 400 head of cattle, his partners agreeing to supervise daily operations.

The following February Roosevelt's wife died two days after giving birth to a

Roosevelt initially stayed in the rustic Joseph Kitchin log cabin on Chimney Butte Ranch, also near Medora. He eventually settled on a place he called Elkhorn Ranch, an isolated spot 35 miles north of Medora.

daughter; his mother had died earlier the same day. Grief-stricken, he quit politics and decided to move out to North Dakota to become a full-time rancher of the open range. The loneliness of the plains suited him: "Nowhere, not even at sea," he wrote, "does a man feel more lonely than when riding over the far reaching, seemingly never-ending plains. Their very vastness and . . . their melancholy monotony have a strong fascination for me."

It took a little while for Roosevelt to be considered much more than a bespectacled, well-heeled, intellectual dandy from back East. What impressed the frontier community most of all was his endless energy and enthusiasm for hard work. Not content to spend his money and give orders, he wanted to get his hands dirty. He might not have had the skill of a cowboy, but he was willing to spend long days on horseback—not only willing, he thought it great fun. His "bully" spirit—the same spirit that would power him up San Juan Hill and into the White House—was infectious, and his adventures became local legends (see sidebar, pp. 138-39).

Despite his hard work, though, the elements were to conspire against not just Roosevelt but all the Northern Plains ranchers. Severe drought came to the region in the summer of 1886. Wildfires and grasshoppers then nearly destroyed the meager grass that managed to grow. Thus already weakened, the cattle had no chance against the winter that was to come. Tens of thousands of famished cattle died in the blizzards and brutal cold. That winter marked the end of the halcyon days of large-scale ranching in North Dakota. Roosevelt pulled out in 1887, but continued coming back almost every year until 1896. Two years later he became governor of New York and led his Rough Riders cavalry unit to victory in Cuba during the Spanish-American War. He would go on to become President from 1901 to 1909, and in addition to his fame as a trustbuster and his "speak softly and carry a big stick" diplomatic style, he is perhaps most remembered for enacting landmark conservation measures—adding 151 million acres to the national forests, creating the national forest service, setting aside 5 new national parks

An autumn cottonwood leaf colors the banks of the Little Missouri River.

and 18 national monuments, starting 25 irrigation and reclamation projects, and establishing the first federal bird reservations and game preserves, which became wildlife refuges.

"I never would have been President if it had not been for my experiences in North Dakota," Roosevelt said. He had come out to see what was left of the American frontier and to push himself physically. Tested by the rigors of the badlands, he found he was made of strong stuff and fit for leadership. The wilderness had left its mark on him, and he in turn wanted to do something for the wilderness. "The conservation of our natural resources and their proper use constitute the fundamental problem which underlies almost every other problem of our national life," he observed. After his death in 1919, local citizens tried to interest Congress in a national park in the badlands to honor Roosevelt. It took until 1946, with land

OPPOSITE | *Students salute the flag at the remote, six-student Horse Creek School in Cartwright.*
FOLLOWING PAGES | *Evening light spreads a ghostly pallor upon chalky buttes in Theodore Roosevelt National Park.*

Ladybugs congregate on lichen, adding splashes of living color to the tawny badlands formations. Although at first some badlands areas seem devoid of life, closer inspection almost always reveals otherwise.

acquisitions following the Depression, for a wildlife refuge to be established in the area; the next year the national park came into being.

Roosevelt's Maltese Cross cabin stands behind the visitor center in the south unit of Theodore Roosevelt National Park, having been moved from its original location seven miles south and then from the capitol grounds in Bismarck. Though small by today's standards, the three-room cabin made of ponderosa pine was considered more than ample in 1884, when Roosevelt had it built. His rocking chair, canvas trunk, and other items give a whiff of the old ranching days.

The more heavily visited south unit features a longer park road, winding through scenery as compelling as in the north unit. One animal you cannot miss here is the black-tailed prairie dog. Numerous prairie dog towns line the roadside, each of them home to hundreds, if not thousands, of animals. They peek out of their burrows, or stand upright squeaking to each other; when approached, they rapidly flick their tails and dive back in. Members of the squirrel family, prairie dogs live an average of seven to eight years.

On little leg-stretching trails through the south unit you can easily get up to

A bee alights on a black-eyed Susan, a common biennial in the grasslands; blooming June to October, it belongs to the sunflower family. Dozens of wildflower species provide nourishment for local insects.

some amazing overlooks. In places you can see terraces of petrified wood, and layers of black-gray lignite coal and reddish scoria—the lignite occasionally catches fire from a lightning strike and slowly bakes until it creates the scoria; one such lignite fire lasted from 1951 to 1977. Another mineral you see—and slip on—around here is bentonite, a gray-blue popcorn-like clay that comes from volcanic ash; it turns into a muddy gumbo when wet. I recognized it as pet litter, but it's used in more than 1,000 products, such as toothpaste, concrete, putty, and paint.

A lot of people like to take binoculars up to the high points and try to spot buffalo and wild horses, imagining perhaps that there still is a frontier. From atop a place like Buck's Hill you can begin to understand why the Native Americans viewed life as a great circle. From here you can see buttes 20 miles or more away; you stand in the middle of a huge circle, some 125 miles around, underneath a vast, incomprehensible sky that domes everything and drops to the very rim of the circle in every direction.

MEDORA AND THE MARQUIS DE MORES

JUST OUTSIDE THE LITTLE PARK-GATEWAY town of Medora stands a house of unusual grandiosity for these parts. The 26-room wooden château was built in 1883 by the Marquis de Mores, a wealthy Frenchman who wanted to establish a cattle empire. He came here at age 25 with his beautiful wife, Medora, for whom he would name the town he founded. His plan was to slaughter range cattle and ship the meat back east in refrigerated rail cars. So he went about buying up land and cattle and building an entire packing plant—slaughterhouse, coolers, and all.

Among the marquis's acquaintances was Theodore Roosevelt, who came to dinner several times and often borrowed books from the Frenchman's large collection. The two men were both aristocratic outsiders and adventurers, but there the similarity ended. For one thing the marquis was much richer than Roosevelt. And whereas Roosevelt was a Protestant New Yorker with a knack for friendship, the marquis was a titled foreigner, a Catholic, and a man who made little attempt to ingratiate himself with the locals. He had a waxed mustache, a haughty bearing, and a sense of entitlement.

At one point the marquis was on trial for murdering a man in a shoot-out over grazing rights. Roosevelt was good friends with a man trying to find witnesses. The marquis wrote Roosevelt, "If you are my enemy I want to know it. I am always on hand as you know, and

between gentlemen it is easy to settle matters of that sort directly." Roosevelt took it as a threat and wrote back, "Most emphatically I am not your enemy; if I were you would know it, for I would be an open one, and would not have asked you to my house nor gone to yours. . . . I too, as you know, am always on hand, and ever ready to hold myself accountable." The marquis apologized, and it never came to a duel, which was lucky for Roosevelt, as the marquis was accomplished with the sword and pistol, having already killed two men in duels.

Though not particularly fond of the marquis, Roosevelt did admire his wife. Medora was not only a painter and pianist, she spoke seven languages and liked to hunt; she undoubtedly drew attention riding across the badlands in her black sombrero and hunting trousers.

In the summer and fall of 1886, the marquis's operation was hit by the same bad weather that affected Roosevelt and all the area's ranchers. Competition with Chicago packers and the marquis's lack of diligence doomed his badlands enterprise. He left before the year was out. In all, he lost somewhere between $300,000 and $1.5 million on his ranching schemes. Roosevelt, who was considered moderately wealthy, lost $23,500, or about 13 percent of his net wealth—somewhat more than the marquis. After leaving North Dakota, the marquis tried building a railroad in Indonesia, hunted in Nepal, organized an anti-Semitic movement, ran for the Paris city council, and fought a number of duels. On an expedition to unify native African tribes in 1896, he was killed by his own guides in the Sahara. Medora made a final visit to the badlands in 1903; after serving as a nurse in World War I, she died in 1921 in Cannes. In 1936 the family donated the badlands mansion to the state. It remains intact, as does the chimney from the meatpacking plant and a church they built in Medora. In fact, St. Mary's is the oldest Catholic church in North Dakota still in use. A simple brick church with a wooden belfry and frosted windows, it is usually open to visitors.

Cyst-like clay-stone nodules emerge from a mud butte in Badlands National Park. These compacted lumps belong to the Brule Formation, a layer some 30 million years old; erosion over the eons has left them exposed.

THEODORE ROOSEVELT

"The joy of living is his who has the heart to demand it," Theodore Roosevelt (1858-1919) once remarked. "The beauty and charm of the wilderness are his for the asking." That attitude of seizing life by going into the wilds was instinct in the young greenhorn dude who came to North Dakota in 1884 with little experience but boundless energy. At first not taken seriously by the rough-and-tumble wranglers, he soon proved he was not one to be trifled with. At one point during that first year he entered a saloon where a rowdy drunk was brandishing a gun and bothering other patrons. He took one glance at the studious-looking Roosevelt and said, "Four eyes is going to treat." Roosevelt tried to laugh it off and go unnoticed. When Roosevelt realized he was going to have no peace, his college boxing instincts took over. His sized up his opponent's stance, then rose and made three quick punches. As the gunman toppled

backwards, his guns fired harmlessly. Falling against the bar, the man was out cold; when he came to, he went down to the station and left on a freight train. The story got around and Roosevelt's tenderfoot image began to fade.

Within his first two years of ranching, Roosevelt had expanded his herds to a total of some 5,000 cattle, making his operation one of the largest in the county. In addition to the Maltese Cross, he established another ranch, the Elkhorn, 35 miles north of Medora and deep in the heart of the badlands. The solitude and peace gave him time for writing, reflection, hunting, and hiking, in addition to the roundups and other ranch work. Some days he spent up to 18 hours in the saddle. "The farther one gets into the wilderness," he wrote, "the greater is the attraction of its lonely freedom." At Elkhorn Ranch, his nearest neighbors were 10 and 12 miles away, and, of course, horseback and foot were the only means of travel. The 30-by-60-foot house had eight rooms and a veranda, where Roosevelt often sat reading or writing.

One of Roosevelt's greatest North Dakota adventures occurred in March 1886. He had just returned from a visit back East and there were still large chunks of ice on the

The Rough Rider President and his wife and children vividly present themselves in this unstilted 1903 portrait. **OPPOSITE** | *Theodore Roosevelt, Jr., poses with a blue macaw in 1902.*

river. One morning his ranch manager told him his boat was missing, the line cut. Despite the bad weather and against his men's advice, Roosevelt decided to go after the thieves. He and his men loaded a newly built boat with two weeks' provisions and headed off in pursuit. Three days later they overtook the men, one of them a known scofflaw and horse thief. After floating downriver for a week, their supplies running low, Roosevelt decided to march his prisoners overland for 50 miles to Dickenson by himself, leaving his two men to handle the boats. At a ranch he borrowed a horse and wagon, hired a driver, and trudged for three straight days behind the wagon, rifle in hand. He triumphantly turned the thieves over to the sheriff and received a $50 reward, then went stumbling wild-eyed out to find a doctor for his swollen, infected feet. He was in a hurry to get back to a meeting of the Little Missouri River Stockmen's Association, which he had helped found and of which he was president. The first man he happened across was the only doctor in the region. Later describing Roosevelt as "all teeth and eyes," yet "just like a boy," the doctor became close friends with the future President. Roosevelt would reenact the episode for photographers, and enjoy telling it over and over throughout his life.

The cornerstone is inscribed "Medora, Marquise de Mores, Sept. 15, 1884" on one side and "Athenais" (her daughter) on the other.

Today Medora, seat of Billings County, still caters to ranchers, and has a seasonal rhythm tied to park tourism. It maintains an authentic old West feel, aided by a backdrop of badlands cliffs. Its Western Edge bookstore, occupying a former motel, is a long building filled with what must be one of the largest collections of Western books available. It carries some 2,000 titles, 90 percent of which are about the immediate region or the West in general, according to owner Doug Ellison. At the other end of town— in other words, three blocks away— stands the North Dakota Cowboy Hall of Fame, which opened in 2005. The organization inducts ranchers, rodeo riders, and basically anybody who has made extraordinary contributions to the "horse culture" of North Dakota. Its galleries limn the richly interwoven story of area Indians, homesteaders, and ranchers.

Executive director Darrell Dorgan grew up in the tiny nearby town of Regent. "I left that life many years ago," he said, "but fortunately ended up back where I started." He travels back and forth from Bismarck, where he runs a historical documentary company and the Lewis and Clark, a passenger riverboat. What was it like growing up in Regent? "It was idyllic. We had race-

horses and cattle. You got to know everybody and a lot about yourself, and no one ever told you there was something you couldn't do or become." In his wide-ranging career, he has fought in Vietnam, reported from the Middle East, and judged and coached professional boxing. At 59, he looks as strong as the ranchers and ropers whose stories he collects. He still feels as though there are no limitations on his life, though he is most passionate about telling the stories of the area's people. "I actually knew people whose parents knew Sitting Bull. These stories were alive for me. This is a wonderful, fragile territory. There's a great regal sense of beauty here and so much history. But it's changing and this is distressing." One thing he points to is the oil industry: "Beauty is not as appreciated as underground wealth."

From the picture windows of his conference room, he pointed out the Château de Mores and the surrounding buttes and breaks. "I respect the people who make it out here," he said. "The marquis gained that respect through fear. His ideas were sound, but he pissed off the other meatpackers. Roosevelt earned respect by riding hard in the saddle, and he became a beloved character."

OPPOSITE | *Tracks in the sandy mud at Theodore Roosevelt National Park, like the area's stone formations, are open texts of events large and small.*

CHAPTER FOUR

BLACK HILLS

GOLDEN DREAMS AND SACRED LAND

Although the Black Hills has a pre-1874 history, the events of 1874 were so significant and long-lasting that everything the area has become can be traced to that point. It was in the summer of 1874 that Gen. George Custer headed out from Bismarck with 10 cavalry and 2 infantry companies on a scouting expedition through the Black Hills. His soldiers were bored after a long winter, and there were rumors of gold in the hills that Custer wanted to confirm. The train of 1,200 men, 110 wagons, and 300 cattle was the first white expedition into the area. Custer encountered few Indians, but did find plenty of gold; the dispatches he sent back to Bismarck triggered a rush. The Black Hills were never the same.

Field glasses used by Capt. Frederick Benteen at the Battle of Little Bighorn.
OPPOSITE | *A bison keeps a wary eye out in Custer State Park.*
PREVIOUS PAGES | *Fun times at the Central States Fair in Rapid City, South Dakota.*

A hawk moth samples a thistle flower in the Black Hills National Forest south of Rochford. The 1.2-million-acre forest was established in 1897 and is thickly covered in ponderosa pine, spruce, and aspen.

RISING WELL ABOVE THE PLAINS OF southwestern South Dakota, the Black Hills are like no other place in the region. Amid the sere and treeless prairie comes a sudden exclamation of granite knobs and outcrops, clad so thickly with evergreens that from a distance the hills look almost black. Sometimes referred to as the Middle Rockies, the Black Hills are a kind of outlying island, with 7,242-foot Mount Harney the highest point in the country east of the Rocky Mountains.

THE PAHA SAPA

SEVERAL GOLD-MINING TOWNS STILL speckle the hills, now thriving mainly on tourism. They were built from the tent cities of miners, gamblers, prostitutes, and thieves that in the 1870s stampeded by the thousands into the Paha Sapa, as the Lakota called the Black Hills. The fortune seekers came in violation of a treaty that gave the Sioux sole ownership of the hills; for a while the army halfheartedly tried to keep the newcomers out, then the U.S. government began making attempts to buy the land. Over the past 133 years the Sioux have filed numerous suits to get the land back, and a story with two sides has emerged. The Sioux, who moved into the area from Minnesota in the early 1700s, say that the Black Hills were

On the alert, a juvenile bighorn sheep shows itself in Custer State Park. Not indigenous, bighorns were introduced here in the mid-1920s, to replace extinct Audubon sheep; about 150 live in the park.

sacred to their people for generations; many local whites claim the Indians were afraid of the area's fierce lightning storms and hardly ever came here before the 1870s, never mind the fact that fear and awe can be the same thing.

In the mid-1970s the Indian Claims Commission ruled that the Sioux were entitled to a monetary settlement; in 1980 the U.S. Supreme Court upheld the ruling and awarded the tribes of the Great Sioux Nation $106 million. The Sioux refused, saying the Black Hills were not for sale. A bill proposed by Senator Bill Bradley in the early 1980s would have returned 1.3 million acres of national forest land to the Sioux, out of a total of 7.5 million that were illegally taken. Though many tribal leaders were interested, the bill died. Since that time, the money has been held in trust by the U.S. government and now totals more than $750 million dollars, with more than $100 million sitting in a separate account in compensation for lands east of the Missouri River. The amount may seem huge, but at less than $14,000 per person, it's hardly enough to make an impoverished people rich. While some Indians joke about what they'll do when they get their Black Hills

FOLLOWING PAGES | *Thumbs of granite jut from the green slopes surrounding Little Devil's Tower in Custer State Park, South Dakota.*

money, others liken the settlement to someone saying, "Here's money for your house, and whether you want to sell it or not it's now ours."

Seen from the air the Black Hills area has a racetrack shape. At least, so it appears to some people. Others, who incline toward the more sacred view, have likened its shape to a human heart. Into this dichotomy pour more than three million tourists a year, intent on roaring around for quick glimpses, or else getting to the core of the Black Hills experience—in either case, they have come to the most prized place in the Dakotas.

On my way into the middle of the Black Hills, I drove a narrow, twisting road up through Spearfish Canyon. Even on a brilliantly clear day much of the canyon is shadowed by high limestone walls. Every now and then Spearfish Creek plummets over a rock ledge, or simply disappears into a sinkhole. On a steep trail off the road, aspens shimmer pale yellow leaves; after a mile the trail ends in a view of sharp ridges and cliffs, exposed like craggy joints above a thick growth of pines.

Well off the beaten track, the community of Rochford is an early mining town that refused to die. In 1896 Rochford's population was 1,100; now a few summer cabins, a gift and antiques shop, and the Moonshine Gulch Saloon are about all that remain. Rochford is not on the way to anywhere—a 15-mile paved road off the winding Spearfish Canyon road ends here. But people continue to come, mainly for the saloon. Betsy Harn, who runs Moonshine Gulch with her husband, has asked people from all over the world how they find their way here. "They get a map and find the smallest dot, and they say, 'Let's go there.' We're not even in the phone book. People tell me they have tourism at home. They come here because they want to see the real America."

Inside the 1910 saloon, the atmosphere at lunchtime is cozy and convivial: Old men drink and talk at the bar, while families and couples eat three-dollar cheeseburgers and bowls of homemade chili in a couple of worn booths; flames dance in a gas stove and beside the pool table a jukebox plays old Western hits. The dark woods and low ceiling give the place a homesteader's cabin feel. The walls are crammed with pictures, memorabilia, an old mining claim; the ceiling only seems low because it's cluttered with ball caps from visitors, as well as signed dollar bills and business cards. "People will go home and say, 'I left my hat in the Black Hills. You go find it and tell me about it,'" Betsy says. "So then that brings them here." As a guardian of "the real America," Betsy agrees that this is the kind of place where people feel compelled not to take a souvenir, but to leave something of themselves, some record that they were here. Even the walls of the bathroom are covered, mostly with high-brow graffiti: "War loves to feed upon the young—Sophocles."

I ask her whether the area has grown. She takes me outside and points down the roads leading to Rochford, which she calls "the last unraped spot in the Black Hills." Since coming here 30 years ago from Aspen, Colorado, she has seen her little neck of the woods swell from a handful of people to nearly 900. Many of them are summer people or hunters, but the area is getting developed nonetheless. The idea of the Indians ever getting the entire Black Hills back is obviously absurd. From Betsy's point of view—and she strikes me as fairly liberal—it's all about the money. "I tell you honestly they never wanted the Black Hills to start with. The Indians are very spiritual, and this is a spiritual place. Lightning strikes here a lot because of the iron in the hills, and they were afraid

Local miner and character Lew Wight still finds gold in the Black Hills, partly by teaching panning and sluicing techniques to visitors. A few companies and hardy individuals still own claims in these hills.

Visions of Easy Street in their heads, old-time panners sift for gold in Rockerville, South Dakota. Very few individuals struck it rich in the mad pursuit of gold, unless they opened up a local business.

of the tremors. All I know is someone's going to get a lot of money. As long as they hold out, they can get more. We're all human beings, I don't care what nationality we are—if we have a chance to possess something we'll do it."

I sit out on the front porch for a while talking to a guitarist who plays here every Sunday to supplement his regular gig at the Four Aces casino in Deadwood. He moved to the Black Hills ten years ago and stayed because of how quiet and laid-back it is. The porch of the Moonshine Gulch is possibly the most laid-back spot of all, and I have to pull myself away to head deeper into the heart of the hills.

A MINER'S LIFE

ABOUT TEN MILES AWAY, UP A DIRT-AND-gravel road, lives miner Lew Wight. One of only four individuals who own a placer mining claim in the Black Hills National Forest, Lew is a throwback in many ways. He greets me in front of his ramshackle trailer, and we sit and talk at a salvaged picnic table. Now 66 years old, he came here 14 years ago for the Sturgis Motorcycle Rally, the end of the road

OPPOSITE | *Gold prospectors churn the dirt near Deadwood in 1876, only two years after the discovery of the precious metal in Sioux lands.*
FOLLOWING PAGES | *Lemon-yellow sneezeweed and coneflowers grace a lush meadow in Spearfish Canyon beneath a light-catching limestone wall.*

after a bitter divorce. "That little red machine over there brought me here," he says. "I spent four months on that bike until I finally found this place up here that looked like it would be my home." So like the miners of old, he quit what he was doing and came here to start a new life. But, unlike them, he had no intention of becoming a miner. It was his natural curiosity about the area, coupled with his background as a treasure hunter, that led him to file a mining claim.

Lew grew up in Virginia and north Florida, then found work with a salvage operator who would become a famous treasure hunter: "I got my sea legs with Mel Fisher as a teenager, finding pieces of eight. Then I was a frogman with the U.S. Coast Guard. I rode motorcycles in Japan, opened up a foreign car service in Hawaii, was the first Yamaha motorcycle importer in the U.S. That was in the early '60s. I ended up growing from there, one enterprise after another—service station, used

Convivial, cozy, and straight out of the Old West, the Moonshine Gulch Saloon caters to bikers, hikers, miners, families, and anybody who happens to stumble upon this 1910 Black Hills institution.

car lot, real estate. But the base was my mechanical skills. Then with my divorce, everything I'd worked for in my life went up like a hand grenade in a trashcan. So I just put myself to work digging in the ground to make me feel good." He leaves the hills once or twice a month for shopping excursions. "Occasionally, I'll stop in a bar and the bartender'll say, 'Hey, Lew, we can't serve you.' Why? 'Cause you're a miner.'" The joke must be a century old around here, but, its pun value aside, telling it gives Lew an identity that links him with the area's history.

Lew talks and moves slowly—he recently survived a life-threatening pancreatic illness—but his mind is overflowing with history and contrarian, independent opinion. His light blue eyes, grizzled beard,

A biker displays his garb and skin art outside the Moonshine Gulch Saloon.

missing teeth, and stringy gold hair trickling from a crusty black cavalry hat suggest a decrepit Custer, which I would discover was not purely a coincidence. While we talk he drinks an O'Doul's nonalcoholic beer and smokes a cigarette, knocking the ashes into an antique can he found.

How do you go about filing a claim? "Same as in the old days," Lew says. "You look at a piece of property on public land, test it, make sure there's gold on it, make sure you're not on somebody else's property. You file it with the courthouse, it's deeded, and you own the mineral rights. You pay a filing fee for your claim, and then it's sellable or transferable."

Do people ever try to mine on his claim? "Claim jumping, yes. It's also called mineral trespass, and it would be like you coming here and going into my Pathfinder and digging through the glove box. It happens all the time. The first time it happens you be nice; the second time you be nice; and then you give them an offer they can't refuse." He smiles benignly.

I ask how he makes out here in the winter. "It's kind of an R&R time. It's not bad up here. The Black Hills is a 90-square-mile hernia in the planet's surface, surrounded by grassland. We're in the center here and we're at high elevation [almost 6,000 feet], but we're sheltered by the mountains around us. So when the weather comes barrel-hootin' from Colorado or Canada, it goes boom and stays down there. We call this the Banana Belt. They get three feet and we get three inches."

Bikers cool off with ice cream at the Sturgis Rally, or Black Hills Motor Classic. Since 1938 motorcyclists have vroomed into the hills to see and be seen; the annual August event now draws 500,000.

After a spirited defense of multiuse of the national forests, Lew delves into an explanation of the area's geology and gold mining history. When he's not digging in the ground, he's mining books for information and has clearly spent untold hours in research. "I understand where the gold is," he says, "why it's where it is, and how to get it. That's not a mystery—the volume and quantity is a mystery, because you never know. In hard rock mining, they can be chasing a quartz vein for hundreds and hundreds of feet, and all of a sudden it's not there, because the mantle of the earth shifted in the Precambrian and things went out of alignment."

In the late 1800s a thriving town called Mystic stood about four miles from Lew's property. "It had a train station, lumberyard, mills, people bustling around what is now my claim. Rochford had 25 hotels and saloons. This area was busier than New York City at noon, with wagons up and down, and a settlement around every curve." Now Mystic is gone, and perhaps two to three vehicles travel this forest road every hour. Lew's claim—about 41 acres—lies at the intersection where Mystic once stood. He believes some 90 percent of the Black Hills gold is still here. "They just scratched the surface," he says. "There's

Modified for racing, parading, and generally showing off, motorcycles of all varieties and vintages show up for the Sturgis Rally, a week-long spectacle and confab of engine-loving rebels.

no such thing as an area being worked out. Watermelons closest to the field get stolen first." The waste area, or tailings, can be reworked with new technology and keep turning up gold.

Lew's main moneymaker these days is his Glory-Hunters business. For a daily fee, he takes hobbyists down to his claim, shows them where to dig or sluice, and lets them at it. "They go down there, kick ass, and take home some gold," Lew says. What they find is placer, or free, gold—ore that has separated from the quartz host and come down the river. Finds rarely exceed two to three grams a day, so at 32 grams per ounce people don't come

here to strike it rich. "It's a big-time national hobby. I have an area that's open-cut, so that when they get there they're not hunting around for gold—they're hitting what we call a pay streak. It's a thrilling experience. I call it Advanced Sandpile 101." Individuals and clubs—totaling 200 to 400 customers a year—come here from countries as far-flung as Japan, Germany, England, Switzerland, Australia, New Zealand, and Canada.

FOLLOWING PAGES | *Like horses of old, motorcycles await their riders outside the watering holes of historic downtown Deadwood.*

Lew shows me some nuggets, chunks, and tiny specks of gold he found on his claim; his earrings are made of his own gold as well. The glittering little pieces do hold a fascination, but gold fever is not what motivates Lew. It's the history he cares about. All around his disheveled lot are pieces of his life and found objects that connect him with the past. He tells me about finding the old Model A truck that sits rusting under a tree, the 50-year-old bank safe, the ore cart. Across the road, his Bobcat excavator sits beside the willow-lined creek where in 1905 a mine operator built a dredge as big as a steamboat— Lew shows me a historical photograph. Behind his woodpile, a 175-foot tunnel bores into a hill, one of countless such holes riddling the Black Hills.

We go inside the trailer, where Lew's much younger girlfriend sits on the bed playing solitaire. A pick and shovel from the old Hope Mine (where his property now sits) are displayed on one wall— given by the grandson of an old miner. Lew also collects antique guns, photographs, and other historical artifacts. He shows me various objects from the 1874

A buck catches the morning light in Custer State Park.

Custer expedition that he found with a metal detector. He studied maps and records and then went out and starting uncovering horseshoes, cartridges, bullets, a belt buckle, and, most telling of all, a crossed-sabers hat insignia engraved "7th Cavalry Co. A." "I was on that expedition," Lew says. I nod, thinking I've misheard. "I was there," he insists. "Whether anybody wants to go with that or not, I rode with them and I remember how beautiful it was." Later he gets out a picture of the monument at Little Bighorn and points to the name of an ancestor, William Lewis. "It's been a lot of fun," he says, "all my lives."

The little town of Lead ("leed") clings to the steep, forested hills to the north. Prospectors with pans and sluice boxes got the town started, but big money left the real mark. Opened in 1876, the Homestake Mine was purchased in the 1880s by George Hearst (father of publishing magnate William Randolph Hearst) and two other

FOLLOWING PAGES | *Splinters of granite thrust from the hills in the Needles area of Custer State Park; an amazing 14-mile road threads this landscape.*

Black Hills Wild Horse Sanctuary

In the far southwest corner of South Dakota, where the Cheyenne River lopes through short-grass prairie, high-walled canyons, and rumpled buttes, wild horses run as free as the untamed winds here. Started in 1988 as the first privately owned wild horse preserve in the country, the 11,000-acre sanctuary is now home to a herd of more than 500 unclaimed horses from the Bureau of Land Management's Adopt-a-Horse program.

Traveling through Nevada in the late 1980s, rancher Dayton O. Hyde was moved to pity when he saw wild mustangs penned up in small corrals on BLM lands. Many of these dispirited-looking horses had been awaiting adoption for years—too plain to catch a horse-lover's eye, then too old, they faced a sad future. Hyde decided to do something about it: He founded the Institute of Range and the American Mustang, which sought acreage for some 10,000 unadoptable feral horses. The Black Hills Wild Horse Sanctuary was the first piece of what Hyde hoped would be a growing movement.

Now, almost two decades later, the Black Hills Wild Horse Sanctuary is going strong, its horses healthy and running the open range. The 500-horse herd is all this delicately balanced grassland can sustain. Descendants of horses that escaped from the Spanish and Indians long ago, the mustangs have never known saddles or riders; grazing free, they add a proud, majestic beauty to the plains. To cull the herd and bring some much-needed income, the sanctuary sells about 100 foals every year.

About 10,000 annual visitors find their way to the sanctuary, which is located 16 miles south of Hot Springs. A nature trail winds from the visitors center down to the bottomland along the Cheyenne River. Guided bus tours travel out into the sanctuary for views of the horses and other wildlife, including mule deer, white-tailed deer, wild turkeys, and hawks. Ancient Indians carved petroglyphs in the canyon walls of this unspoiled country, and Sioux from nearby reservations still hold ceremonies here.

California investors. If you want to know where the Hearst empire came from, go take a look into the gaping crater gouged from a Lead hillside. From rim to rim the open cut measures a staggering half mile, from top to bottom 1,200 feet. But that's not all. Beneath this gigantic wound in the solid rock are 375 miles of tunnels going 8,000 feet beneath the surface. These people were serious about digging gold, and their efforts paid off: During its 125 years of operation, the mine yielded 1,250 tons of gold, making it the leading gold mine in North America. Over the years, the carbide lamps, timber stopes, and compressed-air locomotives of the old days yielded to giant hoists, ore-crushing

Fall color paints Spearfish Canyon in the heart of the Black Hills.

machinery, and high-tech chemical refining, which sifted through an average of 200,000 ounces of ore to yield a single ounce of gold. "Homestake," as Lew told me, was the amount a miner needed in order to call it quits and head back home, which could vary according to his greed or homesickness. The mine was recently picked by the National Science Foundation as the

site of a multipurpose, deep-underground science and engineering lab. With thousands of feet of rock shielding the lab from cosmic rays, scientists will be able to study neutrinos and other subatomic particles.

In a gulch a few tortuous miles to the northeast, the town of Deadwood started out as a mining camp in 1876 and quickly grew into an out-of-control, lawless frontier town of rollicking saloons, dancing halls, gambling dens, and brothels. Wild Bill Hickok and Calamity Jane were among the characters drawn to this free-for-all (see sidebar, pp. 178-79). The HBO series *Deadwood* was based on those early years. The town's Wild West activities went underground to survive the reforms of the 1920s, the last house of prostitution—Pam's Purple Door—not closing until 1980. The entire town was declared a National Historic Landmark in 1964, and efforts to spruce up a somewhat derelict Deadwood began. Then in 1989

OPPOSITE | *Mountain goats find lofty perches near the peak of Little Devil's Tower. These sure-footed climbers take to even the most precipitous cliffs.*

South Dakota voted to legalize gambling again. Since then, the town has prospered like never before.

Main Street has become a mini-Las Vegas of glittering casinos in corniced two-story buildings. Staged shoot-outs happen nightly on the town's brick streets, and a general party atmosphere prevails. But underpinning every ambition and dream here is gambling. Nearly all the hotels, restaurants, saloons, and ice cream parlors have at least a row of slot machines—usually right up front. The major casinos—often jointly run with a hotel—offer free champagne and hors d'oeuvres to get you in the mood for poker, blackjack, and slot machines. Choosing among machines with names like Penny Train, Cleopatra, and Lobster Mania is hard enough. I tried to figure

Reflecting on Mount Rushmore, tourists at the memorial's visitor center prepare to get a closer look at the colossal sculptures; the four presidential visages were carved from the mountain between 1927 and 1941.

out how to play one, asking advice from a tipsy old lady at the adjoining machine, but it was hopelessly confusing. She was too intent on her spinning reels of numbers and starfish and hearts, and there were more lights and buttons on my machine than on the bridge of the Federation starship *Enterprise*.

Along the Black Hills highways, billboards ballyhoo any number of odd attractions that have little to do with the area: Reptile Gardens, President's Slide at Rushmore Tramway, Cosmos Mystery Area, Flintstones Bedrock City. Countering this commercial excess, several designated scenic highways provide unadulterated movement through some of the most breathtaking places in the Black Hills. Probably the most thrilling is a 15-mile stretch called the Needles Highway, which weaves slowly through up-thrust pylons of granite and ends at lovely Sylvan Lake. Among hikes off this road, the one that "gives you the most bang for your buck," as photographer Phil Schermeister says, ascends 720 feet in little more than a mile to a 6,980-foot peak called Little Devil's Tower. It's not for the weak of heart, this trail. The last bit is a scramble across a wind-blasted outcrop of granite to a 360-degree view that takes in Mount Harney, across a ravine to the north, and a Middle-Earthian wonderland of rock spires protruding from a vast forest all around.

SCENIC HIGHWAYS

ANOTHER 15-MILE PIECE OF HIGHWAY, the Iron Mountain Road zigzags toward Mount Rushmore. Along the way it loops, makes hairpin curves, and, best of all, threads through tunnels that frame the monumental sculptures in the distance. There is also a series of rustic "pigtail" bridges supported by logs cut from the surrounding woods. Feats of 1920s engineering, these corkscrew bridges are neither level nor straight, but they do their job of getting cars down the mountain quite well. Road cuts reveal granite, feldspar, and veins of sparkling quartz. And the light tones of aspen and paper birch accent a dark green sea of ponderosa pine and spruce.

And then there's Mount Rushmore. A local octogenarian, who knew the mountain before the sculptures, told me she thought it was wrong to put presidents there. Crazy Horse and his people being from the area, the Crazy Horse monument made much more sense, she thought. But whatever one may think of carving up a mountain, however doubtful it is that a Mount Rushmore could get congressional approval today, the tetra-headed monument is here to stay, ingrained in our national iconography. Begun in 1927, the 60-foot-high heads of Washington, Jefferson, Theodore Roosevelt, and Lincoln took 14 years to carve. Chief sculptor Gutzon Borglum had planned

Cowboys check out bulls in the chute at the Fall River County Fair in Edgemont. Rodeo riding (like powwows and Wild West shows) developed as a way of preserving and showcasing a fading way of life.

to sculpt them to the waist, but his death in 1941 curtailed the project. His son continued until funding dried up a few months later.

Just south of Mount Rushmore, about 73,000 acres have been set aside for one of the country's most outstanding state parks. Established in 1913 as a game preserve, Custer State Park played a key role in the preservation of the American bison, which at that point was nearly extinct. The park bought a herd of 36 animals in 1914, and by the 1940s their numbers had grown to more than 2,500. These giant eating machines were by that point chewing up the park, so a yearly roundup was initiated to cull the

herd, which is now maintained at around 1,500. Signs throughout the park warn visitors, "Buffalo are dangerous. Do not approach." Yet the shaggy beasts prove irresistible to some people. A ranger told me that one woman who'd had too much to drink tried to climb on the back of a buffalo—luckily she was unharmed. Another woman, presumably sober, wanted to get a close-up picture of a buffalo. Too close, as it turned out. The buffalo hooked his horn under her ribcage and threw her; she was in intensive care for six weeks.

You can see buffalo fairly easily from your car. On a recent visit, I also saw a cattle drive along a creek, pronghorn grazing

High-stakes wool gathering: The "muttin' bustin'" event at the Fall River County Fair rodeo on the Black Hills' southern edge gives children a less than cushy ride on the bare back of a sheep.

the grassy hills, wild turkeys along the roadside, and burros standing in the middle of the road. The burros descend from animals that once took tourists up Mount Harney. Other introduced animals include mountain goats and bighorn sheep, though they are pretty elusive; even more shy are bobcats and mountain lions. Prairie dogs and coyotes are somewhat more likely to show themselves, and elk sometimes come into view at sunrise or sunset. Birds frequenting the park include mountain bluebirds, red crossbills, golden eagles, prairie falcons, and western tanagers.

In several areas of the park, stands of trees look either dead or thinned out.

Many are infested with a deadly pine beetle that spreads from tree to tree. To keep the problem in check, the park service clears the dead trees and thins infested areas. Some areas are still recovering from a devastating forest fire in 1988. On July 4 of that year, the woods caught fire after a thunderstorm and burned for five days. Nearly 17,000 acres—$4.4 million in timber—went up in smoke; another $2.1 million was spent fighting the fire. Drought that year caused fires that consumed nearly

FOLLOWING PAGES | *Buffalo still roam in Custer State Park, which holds one of the largest herds of bison in the country—some 1,500 animals.*

700,000 acres across South Dakota and more than a million acres in Wyoming's Yellowstone National Park. Though occasional fires can open up grassy meadows that provide food and habitat for a diversity of wildlife, a new policy of dead brush removal aims at keeping such fires from burning out of control.

Beside jewel-like Stockade Lake at the west entrance to Custer State Park stands a reconstruction of the Gordon Stockade. It was here that a party of 27 gold prospectors spent the winter of 1874-75 in defiance of the U.S. Cavalry, which was trying to maintain the Fort Laramie Treaty with the Sioux. Not counting Custer's unauthorized expedition through the Black Hills in 1874, the prospectors were the first trespassers. Though the Cavalry successfully removed the Gordon party after five months, more whites soon slipped in. Within 2 years, 10,000 settlers had moved into the Black Hills.

CRAZY HORSE

ONE OF THE MOST CHARISMATIC AND mysterious of the Sioux war chiefs was a man named Crazy Horse. Born around 1840 at the foot of Bear Butte, Crazy Horse had unusually light brown hair and light skin. In the mid-1860s he fought with Red Cloud against whites trying to build a road into Montana. Refusing to recognize the boundaries of the Fort Laramie Treaty of 1868, he led his men on hunting expeditions into unceded territory and continued to battle whites and other Indian tribes. With an avalanche of prospectors and settlers brought by the 1874 gold rush, Gen. George Crook attempted to bring the renegade Crazy Horse to heel. Pursuing the chief's band was fruitless. Then on June 17, 1876, on the Rosebud River in Montana, Crazy Horse and his 1,000 warriors ambushed and soundly defeated Crook's army of 1,100. Eight days later he joined with another Sioux unit and destroyed Custer's battalion at the Little Bighorn. Pursued relentlessly after this, he was finally forced to surrender to his nemesis, General Crook, in May of the following year. A few months later he was arrested at the Red Cloud Agency in Nebraska and escorted to Fort Robinson. When he realized he was going to be jailed, he resisted and was stabbed. Refusing to lie on the cot in the adjutant's office, he was placed on the floor. He died that night.

Crazy Horse quickly passed into legend as one of the last of the great Sioux warriors. He never signed any treaties or anything else, never participated in a Wild West show, never left his homeland, never allowed any photographs of himself to be taken, and no one knows where he was buried, although Lakota elders today will say they know. He was quiet and deeply spiritual; his nickname

Bewhiskered Gen. George Crook served in the Civil War before heading out West to fight Indians. Beaten by Crazy Horse in 1876, he forced the chief's surrender the following year.

was "the Strange One." It was thought he was magically protected in battle. His defiance was pure, and he came to represent the wildness and freedom of the Indian spirit.

What better figure, then, for a sculpture that, when completed, could trump even Mount Rushmore? In 1939 Lakota Chief Henry Standing Bear observed the carving of Mount Rushmore and wrote a letter to self-trained sculptor Korczak Ziolkowski ("Kor-jaques jewel-Kuff-ski"), asking him to come to the Black Hills: "My fellow chiefs and I would like the white man to know the red man has great heroes, also."

Ruth Ziolkowski, widow of sculptor Korczak, welcomes visitors to the Crazy Horse Monument. After his death in 1982, she and her children continued the mountain sculpture he had begun 34 years earlier.

That year the 31-year-old sculptor had worked for two and a half months on Mount Rushmore and then taken first prize at the New York World's Fair for a marble of Polish pianist Paderewski. After serving in World War II, he returned and began work on the mountain in 1948. With an almost nonexistent budget, he dedicated his life to the monument, persevering in the face of doubters and anti-Indian sentiment. In 1982, the final year of his life, he said, "I have no regrets. I knew I couldn't finish it. This project is for the future."

His widow Ruth and ten children took over. In the 1990s the 87-foot-tall face of Crazy Horse began to emerge from the granite; it was unveiled in 1998 and claimed title as the world's largest sculpted portrait. When completed, the 563-foot sculpture will top all sculptures and will depict Crazy Horse astride his horse, pointing forward. Ziolkowski was moved by the words of Crazy Horse, who in answer to the taunting question, "Where are your lands now?" replied, "My lands are where my dead lie buried."

The memorial is now a bustling complex that includes a museum, theater, sculptor's workshop, gift shops, and restaurants. I had coffee here with Ruth Ziolkowski one morning, and she told me about the memorial's history and goals. She met her husband in

Connecticut, where she grew up. Of Polish descent, Korczak was born in Boston, orphaned at a young age, raised in a home for destitute Catholic children, and taken in by an Irish prize-fighter. "It was a classic case of child abuse," she said. "His life is an inspiration to a lot of young people—to see how he struggled and what he started. How many people are carving a mountain?" Not yet 21 years old, Ruth moved out here in 1947 to help with the work. Three years later she and the 41-year-old sculptor got married.

"He wanted to right some of the wrong done to the Indians," Ruth told me. "When we first came out here, there were signs in Rapid City that said, 'No Indians served.' And they couldn't vote. Then somewhere in the 1970s, it dawned on him that he wasn't going to live long enough to finish this, and he didn't want

Inspecting the head of Crazy Horse for possible cracks, a worker illustrates the gigantic size of the carving—nearly nine stories tall from head to chin. With only private funding, the unprecedented work continues.

Wild Bill Hickok and Calamity Jane

Among the characters who have drifted in and out of the Black Hills, none were more flamboyant than Wild Bill Hickok and Calamity Jane. Born in Illinois in 1837, Hickok joined the Union Army as a teamster in 1861, but went on to earn his nickname during the war as a sharpshooter and spy. In 1865 he was charged with manslaughter after a pistol duel in Springfield, Missouri. Acquitted, he moved a state west and became a deputy United States marshal out of Kansas.

During the rest of the 1860s and early 1870s, he scouted for Gen. George Custer's cavalry, served as a Kansas sheriff, and continued building a reputation as an ironfisted, fast-drawing lawman, who killed at least five men. It was his predilection for violence that drew both fame and criticism, and only added to the myths about his gun fighting. Standing more than six feet tall, he had shoulder-length, light-brown hair and steely gray eyes. He wore his pistols in his belt, in an unorthodox butts-forward position. Custer's wife wrote of him, "I do not recall anything finer in the way of physical perfection than Wild Bill when he swung himself lightly from his saddle." Custer praised his skill and courage.

Hickok's passion was gambling, and after a stint in Buffalo Bill Cody's Wild West show, he ended up in rambunctious Deadwood, where fortunes were made and lost overnight and the gold-digger and the card player were two sides of the same money-fevered man. During a poker game in August 1876, an enemy entered the saloon where Hickok was playing and shot him fatally in the back.

Although a ladies' man, Hickok likely had no romance with Calamity Jane, as she claimed. A tall-tale-teller, she was born Martha Jane Cannary in Missouri in 1852. From here the facts get sketchy. She almost certainly worked as a bullwhacker in 1879, driving bulls over the plains between Rapid City and Fort Pierre. Whether she was

Unflinching, unforgiving lawman Wild Bill Hickok, in fur hat and necktie, stares a camera down.
OPPOSITE | *Horsewoman and barroom raconteur, Calamity Jane poses with her rifle.*

employed as a scout by Custer is much more dubious, as is her claim of being a Pony Express rider.

Calamity Jane was tall, big-boned, and rugged looking, and her working clothes and chewing tobacco only added to her masculine appearance. Considered a good shot and fine horsewoman, she was perhaps best known as a saloon raconteur whose stories were as outlandish as her ability to put away booze. In addition to riding the range, she worked in more than one brothel, more likely as a laborer than a prostitute. During a smallpox epidemic in Deadwood, she nursed victims of the disease with no fear for her own health. Some said she was protected by her body's high content of alcohol. She was acquainted with Hickok in Deadwood, and her alleged dying wish in 1903 was to be buried beside him.

At any rate, beside him she lies, up in the town's Mount Moriah Cemetery. Their fenced-off graves are decorated with flowers, coins, and stones. On Hickok's grave, some pilgrim left a hand of cards—the aces and eights Hickok had when he was shot, and since then called the "deadman's hand."

to be just another white man who didn't keep his promises. So he started a scholarship fund in 1978. To date we have given away almost $900,000 in scholarships."

THE DREAM LIVES ON

BUT KORCZAK'S VISION INCLUDED MORE than a colossal sculpture and some scholarships: He wanted to establish an entire institution for the American Indian, with a university and medical training center. Now at 81, his widow is still vigorously attempting to carry out that vision. As president and CEO of the nonprofit Crazy Horse Memorial Foundation, she stays busy seven days a week; three of her children work on the mountain, while four others work in the visitor complex.

Since there are no pictures of Crazy Horse, I had to ask if there was a model for that far-seeing face up on the mountain. Ruth told me no one posed for it. Korczak asked several survivors of the Battle of Little Bighorn what the chief looked like. They told him Crazy Horse was small of stature, had a scar on his face where he'd been shot, and had long, loose hair. The rest was the sculptor's imagination. "This is a memorial not just to Crazy Horse," Ruth said, "but to all Indian people. I'd like people to take away from here that the Indians have given us a tremendous gift. Their culture and history need to be preserved."

A guide named Dewey Smith, who retired recently after selling a souvenir shop in nearby Keystone, took me up on the mountain for a closer look at the face. Up close the mica in Crazy Horse's granite chin glints in the sunlight. We walk out onto his arm, which is nearly as long as a football field. "I love working for the Ziolkowski family," says Dewey. "You have to admire them for picking up the reins and carrying on. It could've gone poof, but they each did their part to make sure his dream came true. We all want to feel like we're a part of completing his dream."

So far, eight million tons of granite have been blasted away, the scree forming an apron around the sculpture. Their precision dynamite blasts, which occur about twice a week, can get to within a quarter inch of the finished surface. From that point, pressurized gas torches and other tools take over.

And so the work continues, bit by bit. Children now come with parents who remember coming with their own parents, the generations watching the mountain transform into something spectacular. Here in the heart of the Black Hills it seems certain that the legend of Crazy Horse and his people will live on.

OPPOSITE | *Toots Schriner reminisces in the barn of 12 Mile Ranch, perhaps the oldest ranch in the Black Hills still owned by the same family.*

EPILOGUE

FROM THE MISSOURI RIVER TO THE BLACK HILLS, THE WESTERN Dakotas are a kind of time capsule of American people and places. The prairies are coming back; the broken lands hold secrets of the geological past; small towns are in many places turning to ghost towns. Immigration to this area seems to have left off a hundred years ago. White people still run the motels, restaurants, and other businesses. North Dakota is populated largely by people of German and Norwegian ancestry—the Scandinavian accent carries on like a genetic marker. South Dakota adds Irish and English ancestors to the mix.

For diversity there are Indians. Accounting for about 5 percent of the population in North Dakota and 8 percent in South Dakota, American Indians are by far the largest minority group in the Dakotas. Reservations cover roughly 10 percent of South Dakota's land, with a much higher percentage west of the Missouri. With the reservation system, Indians have a chance of preserving their culture and racial identity, but the result is that there is little visible mixing outside public events such as powwows and school activities. And yet, somehow the reservations grow; the borders between the populations are fluid, and one can almost envision a remarkable day when a majority will be able to claim Native American blood ties.

Windmills old and new turn the never-ceasing winds near Wilton, North Dakota.

Where do the western Dakotas go from here? With a life expectancy of 55 years for South Dakota's Indian men, the reservations need, as Lower Brule resident Sheldon Fletcher suggests, a shot in the arm in the form of investments and economic diversity; the natural resources and talent are already in place. In northwest North Dakota, the answer for now seems to be oil, and more oil. Throughout the region, but especially in the Black Hills, tourism is an increasingly large piece of the economic pie.

In Hot Springs I met a woman named Mary Ellen Duenermann, who grew up on her grandfather's 1892 homestead just east of the Black Hills. Now 85, she remembers the big black clouds of dust and locusts that devoured whole farms in the 1930s. "It was a terrible time," she told me. "But people were tougher then." Perhaps true, but people in these parts tend to be tougher than average anyway. The environment can still be harsh—extremely hot or cold or windy, something to reckon with in a pragmatic, unsentimental way. People are happy to live in harmony with it as long as it gives something in return.

Until a warming climate brings a new wave of settlers, the western Dakotas seem content then to remain America's forgotten place, its last frontier. This region has always asked people to take a gamble—on migrating buffalo, on tracts of fruitless prairie, on rumors of gold, on the future of casinos—and occasionally those gambles have paid off. More often, though, people have just toughed it out, or left. And the wind continues to ruffle the prairie grasses and whistle through the badlands, heedless of the people that come and go.

FURTHER READING

Brown, Dee. *Bury My Heart at Wounded Knee*. Holt, 1970. A detailed history of Indian losses, culminating in the 1890 massacre.

Connell, Evan S. *Son of the Morning Star*. North Point, 1984. Vivid account of Custer and the Little Bighorn.

Frazier, Ian. *Great Plains*. Farrar Straus Giroux, 1989. One of the great modern travel books presents quirky facts and humorous insight.

Frazier, Ian. *On the Rez*. Picador, 2001. Follow-up travel narrative to *Great Plains* focuses on the Pine Ridge Reservation.

Griffith, T.D. *South Dakota*. Compass American Guides, 2004. Excellent in-depth guide with photos.

Horsted, Paul, and Ernest Grafe. *Exploring with Custer: The 1874 Black Hills Expedition*. Golden Valley, 2002. Fascinating guide showing black-and-whites taken during the expedition along with modern shots of the same views.

Horsted, Paul. *The Black Hills: Yesterday & Today*. Golden Valley, 2006. Then and now photographs of Custer, Deadwood, Rapid City, and more.

Jenkinson, Clay S. *Theodore Roosevelt in the Dakota Badlands*. Dickinson State University, 2006. A good, compact historical guide.

Lewis, Meriwether, and William Clark. *The Journals of Lewis and Clark*, ed. Anthony Brandt. National Geographic, 2002. Modernized abridgement of the explorers' journals, with explanatory text.

McCullough, David. *Mornings on Horseback*. Simon & Schuster, 1982. Though somewhat light on the Dakota period, a wonderful account of Roosevelt and family from the Pulitzer prizewinner.

Morris, Edmund. *The Rise of Theodore Roosevelt.* Coward, McGann & Geoghegan, 1979. Pulitzer-winning biography covers T.R.'s life before his presidency.

Neihardt, John G. *Black Elk Speaks.* University of Nebraska, 1932. Sioux holy man's stories form a classic must-read for understanding Indian life and religion.

North Dakota: A Guide to the Northern Prairie State. W.P.A. American Guide Series, 1938. Both a historical document and still-relevant portrayal.

O'Brien, Dan. *The Contract Surgeon.* Lyons, 1999. Fictional rendering of defeat of Lakota and death of Crazy Horse.

Rolvaag, O.E. *Giants in the Earth.* Harper & Row, 1927. Classic novel of Norwegian homesteaders struggling on the South Dakota prairie.

Roosevelt, Theodore. *Ranch Life and the Hunting-Trail.* St. Martin's, 1896. Roosevelt's somewhat turgid sketches of ranching life and local ecology.

Sandoz, Mari. *Crazy Horse: The Strange Man of the Oglalas.* Knopf, 1942. A compelling portrait of the legendary Sioux leader.

Schmidt, Thomas. *National Geographic's Guide to the Lewis & Clark Trail.* 1998. An intelligent how-to for following the trail, with accurate descriptions of scenery.

South Dakota: A Guide to the State. W.P.A. American Guide Series, 1938. Well-written and researched information on the state.

ACKNOWLEDGMENTS

The author would like to thank, in addition to the people mentioned in this book, the following for their help: Fred Walker at the North Dakota Dept. of Commerce, Dennis Neumann at United Tribes Technical College, and Claire Thompson.

ABOUT THE PHOTOGRAPHER

PHIL SCHERMEISTER grew up in Fargo, North Dakota, and spent many days in western North Dakota on field trips gathering plants with his father who was a pharamacologist. He graduated from the University of Minnesota in Minneapolis, Minnesota, with a degree in photojournalism. He was worked on many projects for the Books Division at National Geographic. He and his family live in Sonora, California.

ABOUT THE WRITER

JOHN THOMPSON has written 11 books for National Geographic, including America's Western Edge, America's Historic Trails, and The Revolutionary War. He last covered the Dakotas for National Geographic's Guide to Scenic Highways and Byways. He lives in central Virginia with his wife and children.

ILLUSTRATION CREDITS

All photographs by Phil Schermeister, unless otherwise noted:

21, Smithsonian Institution; 22-23, Library of Congress; 25, Peabody Museum, Harvard University, Photo by Hiller Burger; 30, Yale Collection of Western Americana, Beinecke Rare Book and Manuscript Library 32, Bettmann/CORBIS; 54, Missouri Historical Society; 55 (upper left), Courtesy Independence National Historical Park; 55 (upper right), Courtesy Independence National Historical Park; 55 (lower), National Park Service; 61, Courtesy Detroit Institute of Arts; 76, Courtesy Little Bighorn Battlefield National Monument; 77, Courtesy Little Bighorn Battlefield National Monument; 96, Glen Swanson Collection; 97, Library of Congress; 103, Image courtesy of the National Park Service, Harpers Ferry Center, branding iron in collection of Theodore Roosevelt National Park.; 118, Library of Congress; 128, Library of Congress; 129, Library of Congress; 138, Library of Congress; 139, Library of Congress; 145, Glen Swanson Collection; 152, National Archives and Records Administration; 153, Library of Congress; 175, Library of Congress; 178, Library of Congress; 179, Bettman/CORBIS.

DAKOTAS

Published by the National Geographic Society

John M. Fahey, Jr., President and Chief Executive Officer
Gilbert M. Grosvenor, Chairman of the Board
Nina D. Hoffman, Executive Vice President;
    President, Book Publishing Group

Prepared by the Book Division

Kevin Mulroy, Senior Vice President and Publisher
Leah Bendavid-Val, Director of Photography
    Publishing and Illustrations
Marianne R. Koszorus, Director of Design

Barbara Brownell Grogan, Executive Editor
Elizabeth Newhouse, Director of Travel Publishing
Carl Mehler, Director of Maps

Staff for This Edition

Garrett Brown, Project Editor
Jane Menyawi, Illustrations Editors
Sanaa Akkach, Designer
Margo Browning, Copy Editor
J. Naomi Linzer, Indexer

Cinda Rose, Art Director
Rick Wain, Production Project Manager
Robert Waymouth, Illustrations Specialist
Jennifer A. Thornton, Managing Editor
Gary Colbert, Production Director

Manufacturing and Quality Management

Christopher A. Liedel, Chief Financial Officer
Phillip L. Schlosser, Vice President
John T. Dunn, Technical Director
Chris Brown, Director
Maryclare Tracy, Manager
Nicole Elliott, Manager

Founded in 1888, the National Geographic Society is one of
the largest nonprofit scientific and educational organiza-
tions in the world. It reaches more than 285 million people
worldwide each month through its official journal,
NATIONAL GEOGRAPHIC, and its four other magazines; the
National Geographic Channel; television documentaries;
radio programs; films; books; videos and DVDs; maps; and
interactive media. National Geographic has funded more
than 8,000 scientific research projects and supports an
education program combating geographic illiteracy.

For more information, please call
1-800-NGS LINE (647-5463)
or write to the following address:

National Geographic Society
1145 17th Street N.W.
Washington, D.C. 20036-4688 U.S.A.

Visit us online at www.nationalgeographic.com

For information about special discounts
for bulk purchases, please contact
National Geographic Books Special Sales:
ngspecsales@ngs.org

For rights or permissions inquiries, please contact
National Geographic Books Subsidiary Rights:
ngbookrights@ngs.org

ISBN: 978-1-4262-0317-6 (regular)
ISBN: 978-1-4262-0318-3 (deluxe)

Library of Congress Cataloging-in-Publication Data
on file with the publisher.

Printed in U.S.A.